ON THE LINE
in
THE FAR EAST

ON THE LINE
in
THE FAR EAST

Brian Carlin

Print edition. Also published as an eBook.

Copyright © 2021 Brian Carlin
Cover design © 2021 Brian Carlin & Michelle Carlin
Cover art: an original painting by Paul Seymour

ISBN: 9798738845291
Imprint: Independently published by Brian Carlin

All rights reserved, including the right to reproduce this book or portions thereof in any form whatsoever.

For information or permissions, please contact the author.
Email address: brian.carlin29@gmail.com

Other books by Brian Carlin

Boy Entrant

Kestrel Squadron

Vulcan on the Line (with Geoff Supple)

Dedicated to my wife Pam since much of this is her story too.

Table of Contents

Preface......xi

Introduction......xiii

Chapter 1: In Transit......1

Chapter 3: 209 Squadron......23

Chapter 4: On the Job......31

Chapter 5: Off Duty Life......41

Chapter 6: Sheep-Dip?......51

Chapter 7: Changi......59

Chapter 8: Cheviot Hill......73

Chapter 9: Rose Garden......87

Chapter 10: Rusty......97

Chapter 11: Katong......101

Chapter 12: Work & Play......107

Chapter 13: West meets East......129

Chapter 14: Lessons Learned......139

Chapter 15: Penang......145

Chapter 16: Repatriation......151

Epilogue 159

Photo Credits 165

Acknowledgements 167

About The Author 169

Preface

Labuan was a station to which young, married airmen hoped they would not be posted because it was a one-year, unaccompanied tour that separated them from their wives early in the marriage, and sometimes from young children. Although, in reality it was much more desirable than some other unaccompanied postings. Overseas bases such as Aden at the southern end of the Arabian Peninsula, or the small island of Gan in the middle of the Indian Ocean come to mind.

Singapore, on the other hand, was a "plum" posting. First of all, it was an "accompanied" posting, which meant that there was no separation involved. It was also a "full tour," with a duration of 2½ years, where our servicemen rubbed shoulders with a dynamic, multi-cultural society.

This book is my personal recollection of having experienced both types of posting, and the contrast between the two, both on and off duty. Many servicemen have been stationed at both Labuan and Changi or, in the wider sense, Borneo and Singapore because both had several other bases besides the two at which I served. In many respects, their experiences may be, and probably are, different from mine, which I understand. On the other hand, there is sure to be common ground and I hope that my ramblings will resonate with any reader who also served out there.

After the withdrawal of Britain from "East of Suez" in 1971, neither of the subject postings, nor any others in the Far East, are available to those serving today, so this book might also be regarded as a small "snapshot in time" of one serviceman's experience of that theatre.

Brian Carlin
San Diego, California
October   2021

Introduction

President Sukarno of Indonesia, angered by the creation of the State of Malaysia in 1963, initiated what came to be known as the Confrontation when, by force of arms, he attempted to take over the Malaysian provinces of Sarawak and Sabah in northern Borneo and combine them with the Indonesian ruled southern provinces, to make the entire island Indonesian territory. Both provinces had been former British colonies prior to being included in the newly formed Malaysia.

Because Malaysia had a defence treaty with ANZUK (Australia, New Zealand, and United Kingdom), armed forces from all three countries were drawn into the conflict to resist Sukarno's ambition, with Britain contributing the greater part of the military support. Indonesia was indirectly supported by the USSR and, to a greater extent, by Communist China.

During the Confrontation, the RAF played its part in the conflict by its presence on a few bases in Borneo from where it supported operations by ANZUK troops, backed up with logistical support from Britain's main bases in Singapore.

The Confrontation lasted for three years, from 1963 until 1966, when Sukarno was politically defeated in his own country and a peace agreement signed between Malaysia and Indonesia.

RAF Changi was a more permanent base with a long history. Originally, it was a British Army base in the 1930s era, but when the Japanese captured Singapore during the Second World War, they forced POWs to build two rough landing strips there in a cross-shaped configuration. After Japan's surrender, the RAF took it over and used Japanese prisoner labour to improve the north-south runway for use by military aircraft. The domestic site occupied a large area and even featured a golf course through its middle. The base also incorporated RAF Hospital Changi.

Chapter 1: In Transit

The British Eagle Airways *Bristol Britannia* taxied out to the end of its designated Heathrow airport runway, lined up for take-off and then braked, awaiting Air Traffic's clearance to go. After a few minutes, take off clearance came from ATC upon which the note of the "Whispering Giant's" four Proteus turboprop engines increased as the pitch of the propeller blades adjusted to the angle needed for take-off. Brakes off! At first, the aircraft rolled slowly forward, but quickly gathered speed as it hurtled down the runway, causing the overhead luggage bins and other fittings in the passenger cabin to vibrate with increasing intensity. With a full load of passengers plus luggage on board, it took a lot of runway before the wheels finally lifted off and, with that, the vibrations in the cabin subsided. My ears went deaf, as the Britannia gained altitude, but then popped as I swallowed to equalize the pressure on both sides of my eardrums. Elsewhere in the cabin, children too young to know how to do that, cried because of the painfulness of the experience. It was said that crying was a natural way for the job to get done, but nature never designed us to fly in aircraft, so I doubt it that was really true.

Besides its regular airline business, British Eagle Airways was also chartered by the government to transport military personnel and their families to overseas postings. The charters superseded the earlier troop ships, the passage on which, by all accounts, was an experience better missed.

The date was 9th October 1966 – a Sunday. Passengers on board consisted exclusively of military personnel, some with families and several without. Also, a number of wives were travelling alone or with children, all to be reunited with husbands serving in either the RAF, Army or Navy many thousands of miles away in the Far East. Personally, my service was to be with the Far East Air Force, or FEAF as it was more commonly known. Most of the passengers would end the journey in Singapore, going to one of the many British military bases on the island, but not all passengers. For some, Singapore would be a brief stopover.

I was one of the number of servicemen travelling alone. At that time, a corporal in the Royal Air Force, on my way to take up a one-year unaccompanied posting at RAF station Labuan, located on a small offshore island northwest of Borneo's greater land mass. It was the time of the "Confrontation" with Indonesia. Most of the Borneo mainland was and still is governed by Indonesia except for a small sliver on the north-western edge which is mostly part of Malaysia. This is the provinces of Sabah, and Sarawak, which together comprise Eastern Malaysia. The island of Labuan lies about five miles offshore, close to Sabah's border with Sarawak. The nearby Sultanate of Brunei occupies a small part of what would otherwise be part of Sarawak. The Sultanate is independent of Malaysia but has a defence treaty with Britain.

Several of my friends had already suffered through an unaccompanied posting to that very same station and I was a Johnny-come late because of my tour on the Kestrel Squadron. It was now my turn to be separated from my wife of just 16 months. My other friends had been newly married too, so it was a case of just having to get on with it.

Soon after I had been posted to Scampton in February of that same year, Pam and I had settled in a small, rented bungalow in the village of Cherry Willingham, just outside the City of Lincoln, thinking we would be there for a while. We had also bought a new car, an Austin Farina – well it was second-hand, but it was a big improvement over our first purchase that turned out to be quite a heap, however that's another story. So, it was quite a surprise, or more accurately a bit of nasty shock, to have this unaccompanied posting come around in less than a year after arriving at Scampton. Ironically, the Confrontation with Indonesia had ended by that time, so it seemed pointless to me to have to go out there and so I appealed to the Powers-That-Be to have the posting cancelled. Unfortunately, that wasn't too well received by the P-T-B, and I was told in no uncertain terms to buck up and bugger off out there. So, there I was, on board a British Eagle Britannia, heading off to fight a war that no longer existed. Pam didn't want to live alone in the bungalow and so reluctantly moved back into her parents' home.

**

The trip to Singapore would take around 24 hours with refuelling stops in Kuwait and Ceylon (as Sri Lanka was then known), then a final stop in Singapore from where I would make a separate trip to my final destination by some as yet to be revealed means. Although we were mixed military, every service person on board wore civilian clothes. This was not by preference – it was by edict. Some people in high places must have decided that a load of Brits in military uniform disgorging from a civilian airliner that was making stopovers in foreign countries might just send the wrong message to the inhabitants of those lands. The civvies attire, therefore, was our government's way of not raising any such alarm. Our disguise was further enhanced by the travel documents we carried. My RAF procured passport gave my occupation as a "Government Official." Devilishly cunning – I bet it was identical to the occupational description declared in James Bond's passport and obviously designed to fool even the most astute foreign Customs and Immigration Officer.

Nightfall came upon us quite soon because we were travelling eastward. Sometime later, after seeing very little out of my window, I began noticing an orange glow in the sky ahead of us. Continuing on, points of light began to appear and seemed to be the source of the glow. As we got closer to these lights, it became clear that they were flames, which was when it occurred to me that they were oilfield flares. We were approaching our first stop in Kuwait, even though it took a couple more hours to get there from the time that I had spotted the flares.

Our Britannia was directed into an area that didn't seem to be part of the main airport. The aircraft came to a halt and the engines were stopped. A set of steps was then wheeled up to the door and we were asked to disembark and enjoy some complimentary refreshment. It was a poorly lighted area with some low buildings, but at least it was warm, even though it was late at night in that part of the world. The only facility laid on for us was a counter on the outside of a small scruffy building that reminded me of something you might see at a lay-by mobile transport café. It was there that mugs of tea were being pushed towards us by a raggedly clothed individual. Two other unfriendly looking Arabs, similarly dressed and complete with untidy cloths wrapped turban-like around their heads, lounged outside this little oasis staring at us disapprovingly. Sheikhs of Araby these were not! If anything, they made me feel vaguely uneasy. Because of this, I walked away from them to explore the surroundings - a wide steel-mesh gate set in the wall that bordered the area looked interesting and promised a view of what lay outside our little prison compound. Outside of the gate, a single streetlight illuminated a tarmac street strewn with sand and nothing more. It was a seemingly desolate little corner of Kuwait, so I walked back to the hole-in-the-wall to partake of the refreshments.

While imbibing from a mug of the proffered tea, I got talking to some of the other unaccompanied airmen. Most were also on one-year unaccompanied tours to Borneo, but a couple of them revealed that when they reported for the flight, they were informed that their postings had been changed from Borneo to Singapore and would be a full 2-1/2 year tour, enabling them to have their wives come out to join them. How I envied them.

When refuelling had been completed, we were summoned back on board the Britannia and none too soon in my opinion. Before long, we were airborne once again, wheels up and on our way to the next stopover in the Indian Ocean, several hours away. I tried to sleep, but it was difficult to accomplish while sitting up, even with the seat fully reclined. The occasional onset of the sound of a crying child somewhere didn't help bring the Sandman. The best I could do was doze, then come fully awake, read for a while until my eyes got tired and then go back to doze mode – rinse and repeat.

Continuing our way east, we soon encountered daylight again, so there was something to see on the other side of the window, even if it was only the whirling props or endless ocean, but it made a change from reading. Thankfully, though, as an avid reader, I had brought a couple of books with me and so had ample reading material. There were no in-flight movies or even the means for showing them, no facilities to listen to music or other in-flight entertainment, so it was reading or find some other way to break the monotony. One unaccompanied lad, I noticed, spent considerable time helping the overworked cabin staff to serve meals and pick up the empty meal trays and debris afterwards. I can't say for sure, but it was maybe his way of chatting up one of those ladies back there in the galley.

Some six or so hours after dusting the sand of Kuwait off our undercarriage, we landed at Colombo airport in Ceylon, as it was then known. Nowadays, it is better known as Sri Lanka, except to us old sweats who still refer to it by its former name and the tea that that name conjures up. What a difference to Kuwait! We landed in bright sunshine and in the heat of the day, something that hit me like a very hot, wet blanket as I came down the steps disembarking from the aircraft. By this time, everyone was feeling travel weary, and the time difference didn't help. We were directed to a structure that supported a sunshade and where cushioned rattan easy chairs and tables were arranged. Dark skinned Ceylonese waiters, Tamils as I later discovered, moved amongst us politely offering glass mugs of – you guessed it – Ceylon tea. On their lower half they wore long, white sarong type garments. Looking around my fellow passengers, I couldn't help noticing how pale we all looked in comparison to the waiters and all of us were sweating profusely, especially across our upper lips. Palm trees waved in a warm, gentle breeze on the other side of the single runway, which was not particularly busy.

With refuelling completed, we all wearily climbed aboard again to enjoy the air-conditioned interior of the Britannia and then we were off again on the final leg of the journey – next stop Singapore!

Not too long after leaving Ceylon, night came upon us once again when we crossed the terminator – the twilight zone that separates the planet's daylight side from its night side. The cabin lights were turned off and most people tried to sleep, some successfully and some not. Perhaps I dozed, but only a little. Some hours later, my eye caught a beautiful sight that emerged from the darkness some distance ahead of us. For all the world, it had the appearance of a beautiful, bejewelled brooch gleaming in sharp contrast to its surrounding darkness. As we drew nearer, it got steadily larger until we were almost on top of it. Then, the Britannia's engine note changed, and I became aware that we were slowly descending towards the "brooch" that, in fact, was the brightly lit, vibrant island city of Singapore. Eventually, we passed right over the city at an altitude from which I was able to clearly read the word "National" on a neon sign that flashed on and off to display the logo of the electronics company of that name. Just about then, it was announced, "Please stow your tray tables and return your seat backs to the upright position ready for landing." More new noises as our speed dropped and flaps extended, then the clunk as the undercarriage descended and locked down. The lights of Singapore came up to meet us and then rapidly flowed past underneath as we neared the ground. Next came the runway lights

IN TRANSIT   7

flashing past underneath as we glided to a gentle touchdown at Paya Lebar, Singapore's then civilian airport. It was 24 hours since we had left Heathrow and now late on Monday night because Singapore was 7 hours ahead of Britain at that time of year.

After collecting our baggage and passing through customs and immigration all passengers were directed towards appropriate groups by a KD clad corporal wearing an 'Air Movements' armband. The ten or so of us unaccompanied RAF airmen were instructed to report to another Air Movements NCO who checked our names off a list when we made ourselves known to him. Two or three of our party were then informed that their tour had been converted to full tours at one of the Singapore RAF stations – Changi, Tengah or Seletar. Unfortunately, once again, my name wasn't one of them much to my disappointment. In retrospect, what could I have expected after bucking the system by trying to get my posting cancelled? I can imagine that there was a little note on my file somewhere in Records, where the postings were dished out, that informed the Movements Clerks to make sure I got the "full treatment."

Those of us Labuan-bound were to stay in the Changi Transit billet until our onward travel arrangements were made. As we waited for transport to take us there, the corporal suggested that we get our Pounds Sterling changed to the local currency there at the airport because it would be more difficult to get it done after we left. There was a currency exchange window nearby, so most of us trooped over to it with our traveller's cheques and the notes we had in our wallets. In exchange, we received the equivalent in Malaya and British Borneo Dollars – the currency that was used both in Malaysia and Singapore at that time. Singapore had originally been part of Malaysia after independence but had recently separated from its big brother to go it alone as a City State. A move that was a good one, as history shows. However, at that time, they still shared the same currency, although that would soon change, but more about that later.

It was in the early hours of the morning by the time our RAF bus arrived, but Singapore was still alive as we drove through the streets. Stalls illuminated by Tilley lamps dotted the roadsides as we passed by, but the most notable thing to me was the overpowering smell of bad drains that the wide-open bus windows did nothing to impede. In Singapore, at that time, the monsoon drains were just open ditches into which the citizens just threw their scraps of leftover food, where it rotted and provided food for the huge rats and large cockroaches that thrived in that environment.

We arrived at Changi after having been driven for about half an hour and were taken to the transit billet, a concrete structure which incorporated the bedding store. There we were issued with, not the usual set of six blankets that would have been standard back in home, but just one blanket to use as a mattress cover, a set of sheets, two pillows, two pillowcases and, of course, a mug and a set of eating utensils. When everyone had been issued with their bedding, we were directed to the adjoining transit billet that seemed open to the elements. A dividing wall separated a few rooms with four bedspaces per room. I selected a vacant bed in one of the rooms and made it up with the bedding I had been issued with. Then, tired from the long, mostly sleepless flight, I fell into it in the hope of getting some longed-for sleep. It was a weird experience trying to settle down for a sleep that first night. Large cut-outs high in the external walls passed for windows, except that they were unglazed. This somehow gave me a sense of insecurity. Then there was a smaller cut-out in the wall that separated my room from the one next door (except there were no doors) as though a breeze block had been deliberately left out of the structure. A light fixture was set into this opening so that it gave light to both rooms on either side of the dividing wall. The light remained on all night and attracted insects, which in turn attracted small house gecko lizards that could climb the vertical walls and made a strange "chit-chat" noise. In spite of the experience of being in such strange surroundings I soon fell into an exhausted sleep. Waking up next day – I can't remember what time, but it was late in the morning, it took a few moments to take in the strangeness of my surroundings and realize my whereabouts.

Venturing a look at the outside world that first morning, I was pleasantly surprised to see that the billet was set on a small hillock above a large, football-pitch size area of grassy land, except that what at first glance looked like grass actually turned out to be a carpet of small, broad-leafed plants that seemed to serve the same purpose as grass in providing ground cover. It turned out that common grass does not do well in the Singapore climate and the broad-leaf plant substituted for it. I later found out that the area of land was known as the *padang*, which, in the Malay language, means 'playing field'. Bordering the padang was what appeared to be an area of jungle because of all its tropical trees and vegetation. Best of all was that a troupe of monkeys ran in and out of this jungle, some of which perched on the low wall that bordered the transit billet. This was truly the tropics. The monkeys were properly named long-tailed macaques, indigenous to Singapore, but at the time monkeys were just monkeys to me.

Some of my travel mates were awake and up by this time. One of them suggested that we should try to find something to eat and three of us agreed that that sounded like an excellent idea. I also wanted to somehow let Pam know that I had arrived safely in Singapore, knowing that she would be waiting eagerly to hear from me. There was no email in those days and no other means of rapid personal communication except by telegram, so my immediate concern was to find out if it was possible to send one to her. Telegrams were transmitted by teleprinter and were typically delivered to the recipient by the local post office within 24 hours. Back home, a person would go to the post office and fill out a form with the message they wanted to send. The price was based on the number of characters in the message, including spaces and full stops. I wondered if there was a post office in Changi and if it provided the same service.

We had no idea where the airmen's mess was located, but one of our group suggested that we walk to the main part of the camp. That turned out to be a tall order. Changi was a huge station whose buildings are scattered over a vast area, so much so that a golf course had been incorporated into the green spaces that made up much of the acreage. Walking in the humid heat soon had us sweating and feeling very much overheated and we still had no real idea of where the mess was located. Fortunately, a car pulled over and the driver, a turbaned Indian gentleman, hailed us and asked where we needed to go. Turning around to look, it was immediately apparent that he wasn't just being a Good Samaritan because the words "Sher Khan Taxi" were labelled in large letters along the side of the car. Someone asked how much the fare would be to take us to the airmen's mess and the driver quoted what sounded like a reasonable fare, so we all piled into the taxi's air-conditioned interior and relaxed in its coolness as the driver took us the rest of the way.

It was a long drive and would have been an ordeal had we continued with our original plan to walk. On the way there, the Indian driver informed us that there was a Malcolm Club near the airmen's mess, which was extremely popular with the local servicemen. When we arrived at the mess, it wasn't serving any meals, we were too late for breakfast and too early for lunch, so we took the driver's advice and went to the Malcolm Club and I must say, it was a big improvement on any NAAFI I had ever experienced. There was also a swimming pool in its vicinity, so after getting something to eat and drink, we took another Sher Khan taxi back to the transit billet to get our swimming togs and then went back to the pool. It was very enjoyable basking in the sunshine, but I paid the price in the way of getting a bit sunburned.

Back at the transit billet, I asked the corporal in charge if there was a post office anywhere around where I could send a telegram. He said that there was one on Changi Road, not too far away and gave me directions. It was just a case of walking across the padang to Changi Road and then turning right. The post office, he said was just a short distance along. It was hot walking there, but I was determined to get a message off to Pam, and sure enough, I came upon the Singapore equivalent of a small local post office. The procedure was something similar to back home, so I just filled out the form with my brief message, 'Arrived safely Singapore, love Brian,' filled out the address details and then gave it to the little Chinese man behind the counter. He counted the number of characters and then asked for the appropriate payment, which I slid across the greasy looking counter. Having taken care of that, I felt a great sense of relief, because the need to send the message had been nagging badly at me. Of course, I would write a letter later that day to say all the things that couldn't be included in the telegram, now that I knew the whereabouts of the post office, but for the moment, I could relax a little. And so, I returned to the transit billet to find out what the others were doing.

Everyone posted to tropical, overseas bases were issued with standard khaki-drill uniforms, referred to simply as KD. It consisted of three sets of open-weave, long-sleeved shirts to be worn with sleeves rolled up above the elbow during daylight hours and with them rolled down and buttoned at the cuff after dark. Baggy shorts that hung below the knees; "three sets, airmen, for the use of," in RAF Stores parlance, were for daylight wear, and the same number of long trousers to be worn for night-time duty. Three pairs of khaki, knee length stockings and one "best dress" tunic similar in design to our normal "best-blue" tunic, but with non-reflective buttons. Interestingly, the eagle shoulder flashes on the shoulders were red in colour instead of the pale blue worn at home. There was no KD headgear nor footwear, so our normal home issued hats and shoes were to be used, however the kit included a pair of sunglasses with flexible ear-hooks that made them "one-size-fits-all." The tunic was dead weight – I only ever had to wear it once, and that was for a parade to mark some long-forgotten occasion, but the sunglasses got plenty of use.

Since we were not on duty, we all wore civvies which, in this case, was shorts and short-sleeved shirts with flip-flops as footwear. The whiteness of our legs stood out like sore thumbs compared to the tanned legs of the Changi airmen. Another noticeable thing about the

Changi people was that very few of them wore service issue KD. Instead, their uniforms were made from nicer material, the shirt sleeves were short (mid-upper arm) instead of the rolled up long sleeves that were required with the service KD shirts. The shorts were neat and were a little shorter than knee-length, instead of hanging below the knees like the baggy official KD issued shorts. In answer to my polite enquiry, a friendly airman informed me that the uniforms were readily available from one of the several tailor shops in Changi village at a very reasonable price.

Changi village? We didn't know such a place existed, but that soon changed as it was within walking distance of the transit billet. On my second day in transit, I walked across the padang to Changi Road and then turned left into the village. Changi Road ended at the entrance to the RAF Changi Hospital entrance and the final half mile or so was taken up by shops on either side of the road that sold a variety of goods that, in RAF terminology were "V&A - valuable and attractive" items. All the well-known brand names for luxury consumer goods, such as stereo systems, watches, and cameras were represented as were a number of restaurants and bars, tailor shops, and barber shops. Those were just some of the establishments, but there were plenty of others. I walked along one side until I came to a tailor shop and went inside. The Chinese proprietor greeted me and asked in very accented English something along the lines of, "you want uniform?" I got across to him that I wanted a set of KD with corporal stripes on the sleeve. He then half-heartedly took my measurements, although he seemed to know my size just by looking at me. "Come back in one hour," he then informed me. Time spent window-shopping up one side of the street and down the other soon passed the hour, although window-shopping is not a very accurate description because the shops had no windows and were open at the front. Steel roll-down shutters were used to secure them after hours. The shop keepers, some Indian and some Chinese all tried to entice me inside their shops to sell me all manner of consumer goods as I passed by. "You want Rolex, John? I give you good price." Or "for you, John, a special price." I politely shook my head at each invitation and kept walking until an hour had passed, then went back to the tailor. My posh KD uniform was ready, and the price was ridiculously cheap, so I was happy.

We had been there two or three days when someone suggested that we go into the city of Singapore. It sounded like a great idea, so we called for a Sher Khan taxi. There were four of us and, after enquiring about the cost of the fare, agreed to split it between us. The driver was helpful in that he suggested some things we could do and where to have a meal later. Dropping us off on Queen Elizabeth Walk at the sea front and near the imposing Singapore government building, he agreed to return at a certain time that evening to pick us up again. We had a wander around the area, taking in the sights and at one point, I saw the large neon "National" sign that had been visible from our Britannia as we prepared to land at Paya Lebar. It had been fairly late in the afternoon when we arrived in the city, so it wasn't long before the sun set, and we made our way to the restaurant in the Capitol building on Stamford Road that the taxi driver had pointed out. The spacious restaurant was upstairs in the imposing colonial building, but in the downstairs foyer, we saw a billboard advertising the restaurant that also announced that there would be a Malay cultural performance in the restaurant during the evening sitting. Going upstairs, we were shown to round table not far from the open floor where the display would take place.

Four thirsty young men! The first thing we were interested in ordering was a beer. This proved to be a lager style beverage that soon arrived in pint glasses. It would be my introduction to the ubiquitous Tiger Beer that virtually drowned out all other beers in Singapore and Malaysia, pun intended. The cold drink was certainly refreshing and helped quench our thirst and was a great, if temporary antidote against the warm, humid atmosphere. I don't recall too much about the meal, but the cultural display was certainly enjoyable. A troupe of male and female performers presented themselves on the dance floor, around which the restaurant tables were arrayed. They were dressed in traditional Malayan clothing; the young women wearing colourful costumes that the narrator informed us were known as the *sarong kebayas*. The sarong was simply a long length of cotton fabric that had the two long ends sewn together so that it formed a tube into which the wearer stepped. It was worn around the waist with the loose fabric wrapped around and tucked into the waist to make it fit tightly around the hips, the bottom end coming down to the ankles. The kebaya was a kind of blouse that was tight around the waist, but then flared out a few inches below that. The young men wore white trousers and a white, shirt-like garment that was broken by a wide length of patterned fabric wrapped around their waist like a cummerbund. They also wore a black velvet cap, known as a songkok, which resembled a shortened Egyptian fez, but without the tassel. As I discovered later, this cap was worn by many Malay men in everyday life.

The troupe went about performing various dances and enacted ceremonies such as weddings, all the while the narrator giving us a running commentary on their activities. It was all very interesting and educational and gave me an insight into the people whose country I was now a temporary resident. But, in actual fact, although nominally the Malayan culture was predominant in Singapore, the Malays were only a fraction of its multi-cultural population, most of whom were Chinese, with a small fraction being Indian.

***

In all, we stayed in transit at Changi for that first whole week but were notified on Friday that our contingent of Borneo bound lads were to report to 48 Squadron in uniform on Monday morning for the continuation of our journey to Labuan or Kuching, the latter being the posting for some of our party. Transport would pick us up from the transit billet at 10:00 hours. That gave us a little time to get some breakfast and be back in time for the pick-up.

The bus took us to the 48 Squadron dispersal, where a number of Handley Paige Hastings aircraft were lined up on the pan. I noticed that the unusual squadron emblem adorning the top of each aircraft's tailfin strongly resembled the triangular label of Bass beer. As it turned out, this wasn't far off the mark because I learned shortly afterwards that First World War squadron pilots had stuck Bass beer bottle labels onto their Bristol Fighter aircraft and the red triangular

Bass label was eventually incorporated into the squadron badge, with a Petrel's head superimposed on it, when the Royal Flying Corps squadron became Royal Air Force 48 Squadron.

Chapter 2: Labuan

The flight to Labuan took around four hours in a 48 Squadron Hastings, an aircraft whose designers certainly didn't have passenger comfort in mind when they developed its specifications. This wasn't my first trip in a Hastings and the experience was much the same as before – buckled into one of the hard, backwards facing passenger seats that had only a thin layer of mat-like material to separate one's posterior from the hard metal underneath, while the loudness of its four engines and the accompanying vibration made normal conversation impossible. Dialogues had to be carried on by shouting, mostly between passengers and the air quarter master (AQM), a seasoned male who substituted for the attractive female stewardesses on the British Eagle flight. At least it was a little cooler at altitude after the heat and humidity of Singapore. Little did I realize that Labuan would be even hotter than Singapore.

Ken Brereton, who preceded me in serving at Labuan, and who was repatriated three months before I arrived there, had this to say about flying there from Singapore –

> *There were three classes of service provided for flights to Labuan – Cattle class, Economy class and Business class. It will take little imagination as to who flew in what class.*
>
> *Cattle class: RNZAF Bristol Freighter that was cold, draughty, noisy, and lived up to its nickname the "Bristol Vibrator."*
> *Economy class: RAF Hastings, not as cold as the Bristol Vibrator, nor as noisy, and with the bonus of being faster.*
> *Business class: RAF Argosy, warm, quiet, didn't vibrate, flew faster, and had better seats than the other two, unless it was a combined freight and the passenger section configured with para seating.*

All the above classes featured the RAF's amazing In-Flight Catering Service that consisted exclusively of the white cardboard meal box brought to your seat by Load Master/Air Quarter Master.

After landing, the Hastings backtracked down the single runway all the way to the threshold and then turned into a wide, concrete pan. A marshaller, stripped off to the waist and wearing only khaki shorts, indicated with his marshalling bats for the aircraft to make a right turn and face him, with its tail pointing towards the runway. It was already hot inside the Hastings, so there wasn't too much of a thermal shock on stepping out of the door and down the steps onto the concrete. The AQM directed those four of us who were posted to Labuan towards the Station Headquarters building, one of the small unimpressive, shed-like structures grouped together on the other side of a road that ran along the fenced off aircraft movements area. So, we began to make our way there after collecting our luggage, which had been unloaded and placed on the concrete near the cargo hatch door. The other passengers, who were continuing on to RAF Kuching on the Borneo mainland, hung around the aircraft, taking shelter in the shade of a wing. After our little quartet had passed through the gate onto the public road, I noticed signs on the fence showing a silhouetted figure of a man aiming a rifle with an indication that it was being fired. Words on the sign, in the Malayan language, warned that the area within the fence, which we had just left, was protected by armed guards. No guards were in evidence, but I learned later that when the Confrontation was "hot," my fellow airmen were often posted on guard duty with an unloaded rifle and a few rounds of ammunition that could be loaded into the weapon and fired only on the express orders from much higher authority.

At SHQ, we found the Orderly Room, which wasn't difficult in the small building, and made ourselves known to the clerk. He soon made the necessary annotation in his records and handed each of us the familiar blue arrivals card and directed us to the nearby bedding store. There weren't too many signatures to obtain on the blue card –

no luxury sections such as a bicycle store on the station and the camp was quite small, so the arrivals process could be easily expedited, and there wouldn't be too much walking around, which was a blessing in such a hot environment. The bedding store was our first stop, because we needed a place to lay our heads that night. The bedding we received was identical to that which we had been issued at Changi, except for the addition of one other strange gauzy item.

"What's this?" One of our party asked.

"That's a mosquito net," replied the bedding store clerk with a wide grin, then added, "You're going to need it here."

In fact, we knew that we were now in a region where malaria was endemic and prior to leaving Scampton, the Medical Officer had issued me with a course of Paludrine tablets to begin taking before leaving home in order to build up the level of the drug in my system. This was an anti-malarial drug that was supposed to protect against being infected with the disease. I was strongly advised to take a daily dose of Paludrine once I arrived on Labuan, but how to do that wasn't clear because I only had enough tablets for a few days and the supply was running out fast. However, it wouldn't be too long before I found out the simple solution to this dilemma.

Our first priority, as new arrivals, was to find the transit billet where we could claim a vacant bed and dump our bedding and luggage. The bedding store clerk kindly offered to show us where it was because, he said, he was going that way anyway. The billets were on a slightly lower level than the airfield and administrative part of the camp, so the helpful clerk guided as down a short incline and then turned right onto a camp street that had a row of what looked like corrugated chicken-farm sheds along one side. I noticed an airman approaching us from the opposite direction, eying us with a nasty smirk on his face. As he came abreast of us, he mockingly commented, "You'll get your knees brown out *here* lads!" I soon learned that newly arrived people were known as "moonies" – a derogatory term that compared our lily-white skin to that of the pale, full moon.

We walked a little further along the road until our guide indicated one of the chicken-farm sheds as the transit billet. If the one at Changi was outside of my normal experience, this one was light-years beyond it. The roof was of corrugated metal, but there were no walls. Instead, a second level of corrugated sheet metal was attached to the hut uprights midway between the ground and the roof edge, like a ballet dancer's skirt, having the same slope angle as the roof (see photo). The billet, or "basha" as the design was known, appeared to accommodate around 20 occupants.

Inside the billet, and I use the word "inside" loosely because the structure was open to the elements on its two long sides, I dumped my bedding and the suitcase that held my clothing and other essentials onto a vacant bed. Then, together with the others, went back up the slope to continue the "arrivals" process by reporting to a number of sections in a certain order, as designated on our "blue chit" arrival cards. At each section, the chit was signed by someone with the authority to do so, while our name, rank and service number were entered into that section's nominal roll. One of the stops was Station Sick Quarters where we learned that Paludrine was available on a self-serve basis in the Airmen's Mess, so that was that problem solved. Another important signature was the section to which I was internally posted. This turned out to be the 209 Squadron detachment from RAF Seleter in Singapore. The squadron admin office was located in the small hangar at the edge of the pan where the Hastings had dropped me off earlier. An orderly in the office signed my blue chit and instructed me to report back there the next day when I had finished "arriving." The three other newly arrived lads had gone off to their respective sections, and now being on my own, I continued my rounds of the prescribed sections collecting the required signatures.

After having completed the arrivals process, I made my way back to the "basha" hut that would be my home for at least one night and went about making up my bed. That part of the task was easy – I had done it a million times, but what to do with the mosquito net? Looking around at the other bed spaces, I saw that the other lads had attached one end of the net to a hook embedded in a horizontal wooden rail that was the attachment point for the corrugated metal roof skirt. It also doubled as a convenient place for the "mozzy" net hooks, one each of which had been placed above each bed. I attached my net to the hook over my bed, using ties on the end of the net that were obviously for that purpose. One by one, the three others straggled in, having finished getting all signatures on their blue chits. They too made up their beds and dealt with their own mosquito nets, sometimes with a little guidance from yours truly.

By then, being late afternoon, it was time to go to the airmen's mess for something to eat, so the four of us set off walking towards the mess along the street that fronted the billets. Along the way, we saw that one of the huts actually served as a shop operated by an Indian man and a young girl, presumably his daughter. The man wore a colourful sarong, while the girl wore the traditional Indian sari. The shop appeared to sell a variety of non-food items and gave the impression that it might be a handy place to buy some sundry items. It certainly merited a visit later.

The airmen's mess was in a little tree sheltered area, so it was relatively cool, although open-sided like the billet we had just left. Along the side of the servery, where we queued up, I spied a bowl containing a quantity of pills. As the men in front of us in the queue shuffled past the bowl, on their way towards the serving area, most dipped a hand into the bowl and took one of the white pills. This, it seemed was where we were able to get our daily dose of Paludrine. I don't recall what the food in the mess was like, but it was most likely standard RAF fare with a little local food thrown in.

The sun was low on the horizon by the time we made our way back to the billet and would set at 6 pm, give or take a minute or two. Twilight lasted a noticeably short time and within a quarter of an hour full darkness had descended. Being so near to the equator, there was virtually no seasonal difference in the time that the sun rose and set with almost equal division between the hours of daylight and those of darkness. It also set very quickly – I could actually see it moving downwards towards the horizon.

It had been a long day, and I felt tired out, so decided to get washed and go to bed, both of which proved to be out of the ordinary experiences. The ablutions, as I soon discovered, were housed in a corrugated metal-clad structure outside the billet and served two or more of the nearby huts as well as the transit billet. It was dimly lit and contained the usual toilets, urinals, washbasins, and showers. The main difference between these ablutions and all others that I had experienced, with the exception of summer camp when I was a boy entrant, was that they featured cold water only. Not that that was a great hardship given the ambient temperature. In fact, it could be described as refreshing, except for shaving, which really calls for hot water. But that evening, I didn't need to shave, so a shower was more in order to wash off the sweat of the day.

Going to bed was much stranger than the ablutions experience. Beds in the billet were arranged in normal barrack room fashion with the head of the bed towards the wall and the foot towards the centre aisle. The only problem was that there was no wall there! I was looking directly at the ground outside. The only thing that blocked my horizontal view was the corrugated metal skirt on the other side of where the wall would have been, had I been back in civilization. Adding to that, I now had to deal with the mosquito net. Undoing the folded-up fabric, I draped it over the bed, making sure it hung down all the way around and that there were no gaps. Then I got into bed. So now I was inside this white, gauzy net in a structure that was essentially open to the elements. Several ceiling fans spaced along the length of the billet whizzed around at full speed, billowing the net and those of all the other occupied beds, making the whole situation somehow surreal. The absence of a wall concerned me the most, engendering a strong feeling of insecurity. Worse – a thunderstorm passed directly over the camp in the middle of the night. Deafening booms of thunder, interspersed with loud, ear-splitting cracks that had me imagining the heavens splitting open, and brilliant, prolonged flashes of lightning, all accompanied by torrential rainfall that beat a tattoo on the metal roof overhead and then cascaded noisily down onto the metal skirt right outside, no more than three feet from my head. The drumming of the heavy rain on the skirt also added to the din, altogether making sleep impossible while it lasted. At least we stayed dry inside, so the roof skirt seemed to be doing its job, although I could feel a fine spray of moisture on my face generated by the rain bouncing off the metal skirt. What I would discover in the following weeks was that nightly storms like this were a regular occurrence.

Shortly after the noise of the storm had faded into the distance, and peace returned to the billet, an intruder within my mosquito net made its presence known, announced by the irritating, high-pitched whine of its wings every time it came near either of my ears. Try as I might, I couldn't locate it and suffered a few bites that were visible as itchy red bumps in the morning. Too late, I remembered the advice of someone, maybe the bedding store clerk, who had warned we newcomers to make sure our net was tucked in under the mattress all round, otherwise the little buggers could get inside while you slept. The only way to make sure of that was to tuck it in before getting into the bed, just leaving a small opening large enough to crawl through and then tucking that last part in once inside the net. Next night would be different, I promised myself.

Chapter 3: 209 Squadron

Next morning, after breakfast, I reported to SHQ, having completed the "arrivals" process, and was told to report to the 209 Squadron Orderly Room. Walking there, I noticed that all the erks working on the pan and in the hangar were stripped off from the waist up and most of them were as brown as the proverbial berries. By this time, I had the beginnings of a tan, having gained it the week before at the swimming pool at Changi, but it was nowhere near as deep as my soon-to-be fellow squadron members.

After reporting to the SNCO in charge and being made welcome and advised to move into one of the squadron billets, which were some distance away from the transit billet, I was taken to the crew room and introduced to the current occupants. Before returning to his office, the sergeant detailed one of the lads to show me to the billet where I was to move my bedding and personal belongings when we knocked off work at the end of the workday. Like those working outside, everyone in the room was stripped off to the waist and I couldn't help but notice that the comfortable, cushioned, well used "easy" chairs with which the crew room was furnished were all heavily soiled from the grimy sweat stains of the squadron members. Looking around at the faces, I recognized a couple that were familiar. One was former Boy Entrant Adam-Smith who had been a fellow billet member while we were both in training at RAF St. Athan in South Wales. The other was Ron, a former colleague in the Scampton Electrical Bay who had preceded me to Labuan by several months. Both lads were near the end of their one-year tour and would not be around for very much longer, so it was almost a hello-goodbye situation.

The squadron at Labuan was actually a small detachment from the parent squadron at RAF Seleter in Singapore, which was 209's home base. The detachment was comprised of five Scottish Aviation

Pioneer aircraft. Two of them were Twin Pioneers and the other three were Single Pioneers. The "twin" and "single" designations referred to the number of engines with which each type was equipped. No prize for correctly guessing which was which! We rarely, in fact, we never referred to them as Pioneers, but always as "Pins" – Twin Pin and Single Pin. The squadron also had charge of two Vickers Valettas, which I think may have belonged to number 52 Squadron based at RAF Kuching on the Borneo mainland, although that particular squadron had disbanded in April of that year, six months before my arrival, so we probably just looked after them until such times as a new home was found for them. They flew, though, and were mostly crewed by NCO aircrew.

Just as an aside, 209 squadron had an interesting history that went all the way back to the First World War when it was a Royal Flying Corps squadron, which then became a Royal Air Force squadron when the RAF was formed on April 1, 1918. Its greatest claim to fame was that, during the conflict and a mere three weeks after the formation of the RAF, one of its pilots, Captain Brown, a Canadian, shot down the notorious Red Baron von Richthofen, seriously wounding him and forcing him to land in a nearby field where he succumbed to his wounds shortly after a small party of Australian soldiers arrived at the scene of the crash. In recent years, that claim has been challenged and it has been postulated that the German ace was actually brought down by an Australian soldier in the trenches. This counter claim is based on the angle of the bullet's path through Richthofen's torso. Despite the controversy, the 209 Squadron badge incorporated an image of a bird, all red in colour and supposedly an eagle, head pointing downward, and its wings swept backwards as it appears to plummet earthwards. This, of course, represents the Red Baron's final dive to the ground. Typical of "other ranks" irreverence, we often referred to the red eagle symbol as the dying duck!

That first day seemed to fly by as one of the other electricians familiarized me with the Pins and the Vallettas. After working on Vulcans, the Pins we're a piece of cake from an electrician's point of view – at least this electrician's point of view. According to my colleague, faults were few and far between and, even then, amounted to little more than failed bulb replacement and other simple things. There was always routine maintenance to carry out, such as changing the batteries on the typical two-week cycle for the lead-acid variety, and minor inspections whenever the airframe achieved the number of flying hours that triggered this level of servicing. So, it was mostly a matter of pre-flight, post-flight and turn-round inspections that exercised my professional expertise as well as general flight-line duties such as starter and seeing-in crew, although, unlike being on a Vulcan squadron, the crew typically consisted of just two men. However, the squadron also acted as the de facto Station Flight and was therefore responsible for receiving and handling all visiting aircraft large or small. That's what lent the job some variety and interest. We also shared the aircraft movement area – the pan – with Malaysia-Singapore Airlines (MSA), as it was then known (later, the two broke up into separate entities, one being Singapore Airlines, while the other became the Malaysian Airline System), but the only MSA aircraft we saw was an ancient DC3 Dakota that plied between Labuan and destinations on the Borneo mainland – Brunei, Jesselton (now renamed Kota Kinabalu) and Kuching.

When it came time to knock off for the day (no night shift, which was good news), I accompanied Paul, who had been "volunteered" to show me the location of my new digs. He was one of the lads who lived in the billet to which I had been assigned. When we arrived there, I was relieved to find that it was more like a traditional billet with actual walls punctuated with windows. I should say window openings, because they weren't glazed, but had louvered shutters hinged on the outside, which could be closed to offer some protection from the elements. Like the basha huts, however, the roof was of shiny, corrugated metal. Inside, the beds were all neatly made up and mosquito nets neatly tied up in bundles which were attached to hooks on the wall above each bed. The billet also seemed clean – the floor had obviously been swept and waste bins didn't contain any rubbish. I must have remarked on this, because Paul informed me that the billet members jointly employed a local house boy to make their beds, change the sheets on laundry day, and keep the billet clean. He also came in the evening to deploy the mosquito nets before it got dark, which was when the little buggers became most active. Each billet member had to make their own arrangement with the house boy and paid him weekly, but the amount he asked for was really just a pittance and seemed well worth the outlay.

After collecting my bedding and the small case that contained my clothes and personal belongings from the transit billet, I returned to my new billet and was surprised to see that Paul had changed from his work KD and was now clothed from the waist down in a full length, brightly coloured sarong. Although I didn't say anything, the get-up struck me as being a little effeminate, instead I just set about making up the bed I had selected from the few available vacant ones in the billet. Others had entered the billet by now and mugs and irons (eating utensils to the uninitiated) were being grabbed as some of them obviously intended to head to the mess for their evening meal. Someone asked if I was coming, so I grabbed mine and went with them. After we had all got our meal and were sitting at a table, someone mentioned about going to the NAAFI afterwards for a beer. Everyone seemed to be in favour although, being the new boy, I didn't say anything, but then the same person who had originally invited me to eat with the group smilingly asked if I wanted to join them. Wanting to be accepted into the group, I of course agreed and so, after dropping our mugs and irons back at the billet, we all walked the short distance to the NAAFI. The camp was quite compact, so nothing was very far away. For a couple of hours after that, I chugged down a few cans of Tiger beer and enjoyed the jokes, leg pulling and the otherwise great camaraderie that ensued. At the same time, I picked up some tips on the work environment and life in the billet. At one point, I told someone about the little night-time visitor inside my mosquito net the previous night and asked how to avoid it from happening again. Others quickly joined in on that conversation and the unanimous opinion was that the net needed to be tucked in under the mattress all the way around. This was something the house boy did in the evening, as part of his service. Of course, not having made an arrangement with him, my net was still how I had left it, so when I got back to the billet, the first thing I did was untie it and tuck it in. The house boy was there – a local young man, apparently in his late teens or early twenties. He looked my way briefly, once or twice, but didn't say anything nor did I say anything to him. Did I really need his services, I asked myself?

One other thing I should mention is that, on returning to the billet, I noticed that many if not most of the other lads were now clad in sarongs. So, I had apparently misjudged Paul and now realized that he wasn't really effeminate, and that the sarong appeared to be the dress of choice in and around the billet. I wondered if it was just a fad, but again, reality reared its head when itchy red lumps started erupting on my ankles and calves. They had seemingly become a snack bar for the local mosquito population. And that's when the penny dropped as to why so many of the lads wore sarongs. It was to keep the mozzies off their legs, which apparently was the insect's favourite target.

My sleeping experience turned out to be much better than it had been the previous night because no mosquitoes penetrated my defences. It was also because I now felt more secure in a building with walls. The "four walls" thing was purely psychological, I know, but that's how it felt. There was an opening, just below the roof line, along the length of the billet that allowed air to circulate, helped by the four ceiling fans that were running full blast. The draught from the fans wafted the mosquito nets enveloping all the occupied beds, causing them to billow and undulate continuously, thereby creating a surreal, ghostly scenario in the dim, ambient light.

The next morning, after a cold-water shower and cold-water shave, followed by breakfast in the airmen's mess, I made my way to the 209 squadron hangar, leaving my bed unmade in the hope that the house boy would make it up. Reality kicked in when I returned to the billet at lunchtime to find all beds made and mosquito nets neatly stowed – all that is except mine. The house boy was still hanging around the billet, so this time I approached him with the thought of having him take care of my bed and keeping my bedspace swept. He readily agreed to include me in his services and to seal the deal I proffered the going weekly rate of one Malayan Dollar, which was a good bargain, the dollar being worth 2 shillings and fourpence (2/4^d) in pre-decimal British currency, or 12p post-decimal. The service was excellent, although the price unfortunately also included being subjected to the embarrassing comments he occasionally directed towards his "employers." I just might reveal more about that later.

That evening, on my way back from work, I called into the little Indian shop near the transit billet and purchased a sarong.

Twin Pioneer

Single Pioneer with 209 Sqdn. emblem on the tail

Chapter 4: On the Job

One of my first jobs at work was to learn the drill on how to see off a Single Pin. The airman providing the lesson advised me to grab a cleaning cloth from stores and bring it with me. When I asked why, he replied with a knowing smile, "You'll see."

The seeing off process was fairly simple – bring a fire extinguisher near the aircraft, "just in case," and to extend the wheel-chock pull chains fully out to each side of the aircraft so that they could be pulled away without having to get into the propeller backwash. The other task that I was shown was how to load the Coffman engine starter breech with six cordite cartridges, or at least add enough to make up that number if it already contained some. That was something I was actually familiar with, having performed the same thing many times when I worked with Chipmunks at Cranwell, but I kept that to myself. It wasn't necessary to assist the pilot to strap in because there was ample room for him to do so by himself and since the Pioneers didn't have ejection seats that needed to be armed after the pilot had strapped in, our job didn't require us to go inside the aircraft. So, both of us waited a short distance ahead of the port wingtip while the pilot did his pre-start checks before giving the thumbs up as the "ready to start" signal. A quick look around to make sure everything was clear and then my mentor returned the signal. There followed a quick puff of white smoke as the Coffman cartridge fired and exhausted through a small port on the side of the engine housing. Almost immediately, the propeller spun at an incredibly fast speed as then, one by one, the radial engine's cylinders fired. Much more smoke belched out from under the engine cowlings and was immediately blasted backwards by the wash from the prop. The engine then settled down and the aircraft rocked in sympathy with the engine's rhythm. At this point, the other groundcrew man strode under the wing, well clear of the rapidly spinning prop, and with one hand, pulled a rag from his pocket while, with the other, he grabbed a handhold at the side of the cockpit and stepped up onto the top of the undercarriage wheel. What I hadn't noticed was that when the engine started, the smoke that billowed out from under the radiator cowlings was accompanied by a heavy shower of engine oil that had leaked from the radial engine cylinders. Much of this was deposited on the cockpit windscreen and now my mate was busy wiping it off so that the pilot could see where he was going. His advice about bringing a rag when seeing off a Single Pin then became clear. With the windscreen clear, the pilot gave us the "chocks away" signal and was then marshalled out onto the pan, from where he taxied out to the runway and was airborne within what seemed to be just a few feet.

The Scottish Aviation Pioneers, single and twin, were remarkable aircraft in their own way. While not possessing particularly attractive lines, their airframe was designed to be able to deliver a small number of passengers or cargo into a ridiculously small, restricted area. For this reason, it possessed both flaps and slats. The former were large in area when compared to the relative area of the main wing. The latter slats lay along the top of the wing leading edge and could be lowered to change the aerodynamic geometry of the wing, giving it greater lift at slow airspeed. Lowering the flaps by a few degrees also had the same effect, so the flaps and slats, when employed together gave the pilot the ability to safely land the Pioneer at a very slow speed and thus in a very short landing area. The same geometry also gave the aircraft the ability to take off after a truly short take-off run. Some said that certain pilots could get the aircraft airborne within its own length and I don't doubt that, given a decent headwind. Thus, its designation as a STOL aircraft (**S**hort **T**ake-off **O**r **L**anding) was accurate. Unfortunately, I never had a flight in either of the Pins. This was due mainly to my own stubbornness – I had vowed to myself that the only time I would ever fly from Labuan was the one on which I would begin my homeward bound journey. As it was, my stay there was short and I now believe that had I done my full one-year tour there, I would have eventually discarded that resolution and enjoyed some of the trips to such places as Jessleton that some of the other lads experienced.

Slats and flaps deployed

The Royal Malaysian Air Force also shared the same base – in fact, it was their base, and we were just temporary guests. The RMAF operated De Havilland Caribou aircraft, which were quite a bit larger than either of the Pioneers. It was a treat to watch them land, located where we were near the end of the runway threshold, because they too were STOL aircraft that could land almost in their own length.

As part of our transit aircraft handling duties, we received a 48 Squadron Hastings each weekday. This was the same flight that brought me out to Labuan, and I learned that it was referred to as the CHALK. This was an acronym for Changi-Labuan-Kuching because it was a daily "milk run" between the three stations, transporting personnel, incoming and outgoing mail and various supplies and aircraft replacement components. I soon began looking forward to the CHALK because it brought letters from Pam. We had agreed to write to each other every day, so most days I received a letter and was sorely disappointed on the rare days when the CHALK let me down.

Argosy transport aircraft were also frequent visitors. Their four Rolls Royce Dart engines ran at constant speed, even when taxiing and they, or more likely their propellers, gave off a loud, high pitched whining sound that was uncomfortable for ground crew in the vicinity. The small black radome at its tip gave the dome-shaped nose the appearance of a female breast and, for that reason, coupled with its high-pitched propeller noise, earned it the nickname "The Screaming Tit" amongst the ground crew fraternity.

A "Screaming Tit" Argosy

    While we worked out on the pan on any given day, the Malaysian-Singapore Airlines DC3 Dakota made frequent arrivals and departures, using the civil airport's share of the pan. Typically, it entered the pan at an entrance near the control tower, which also housed the civil terminal. It then swung around so that its nose pointed towards the tower and its tail faced towards our end of the pan. On one occasion, we were performing an engine run on one of the Twin Pins, probably to test a replaced generator. The Twin Pin was positioned at the very edge of the area assigned to the RAF, which bordered on the civil end. While we were engaged in running the engine, the DC3 landed and taxied to its usual parking spot and, in doing so, its tail and the Twin Pin's tails ended up facing each other. There was still quite some distance between them, but apparently not enough. During one full rpm run of one of the Twin Pin's engines, the propeller blast blew the DC3's rudder off, much to the outrage of the MSA people. While I understood their anger, it also seemed that the incident may have saved the lives of future passengers and crew because, if the rudder could be blown off by the backwash of propeller at some distance away, what were the chances that it was on the verge of coming off in the air?

The photograph below is by courtesy of the North Borneo Historical Society. It gives a wide view of the entire pan in the 1963 – 1965 period, including the control tower and civilian air terminal in the foreground. The MSA DC3 is parked facing into the pan at the near left corner. Beyond the DC3, a Twin Pioneer can be seen, with the edge of our hangar between the two. A Valletta is parked beyond the Twin Pioneer. The headquarters and other administrative buildings can be viewed on the extreme left of the picture. On the right of the picture, the two Beverleys are easy to recognize, as is the Javelin, and I'm fairly sure the Javelin's neighbour is a Pembroke.

The old airport terminal c. 1963-65 **LABUAN**

On one occasion, a Transport Command Britannia landed to refuel. The Air Quarter Master came out and joined a few of us who were on the seeing-in crew. He said that all his passengers needed to come out for some fresh air and to stretch their legs. The aircraft was transporting a full passenger load of Ghurkhas with their wives and children. I don't know where they came from or where they were going, but it seemed that they had been airborne for some time.

As for the Ghurkhas – they are legendry jungle fighters and certainly not the kind of people you would want to meet up with in the jungle if you were on the opposite side. There are many stories about them although I don't know if they are all completely true. There's one about when they were fighting in Burma during the Second World War. Supposedly, they hid in the undergrowth alongside jungle trails and when troops came along the trail, they would surreptitiously reach out and feel the person's boot laces. If the boots were laced in criss-cross fashion, they knew that the wearer was a Japanese soldier who was then quickly dispatched by the Gurkha's kukri – the fearsome curved weapon that they kept well sharpened for use not only as a weapon but to use in chopping through jungle undergrowth.

One other story I heard, which was relevant to the Confrontation, is that a Gurkha patrol came across a *kampong* (native village) where a football match was under way on the village padang. It seems that one side consisted of Indonesian soldiers and the opposing team was made up of Malaysians. That's understandable in a way, because the Malaysians and Indonesians are basically the same race and speak a common language, so perhaps they decided to settle their differences in a sportsman-like manner. The story goes that the Gurkhas didn't spare anyone from either team.

But although the Ghurkhas have a reputation for being fearsome fighters, when they deplaned from their Britannia onto our pan that day, they seemed to be of a mild disposition and were very respectful towards us. Appearances can be deceptive, I suppose. One thing that is true about them, however, is that they received a daily rum ration and, on one memorable occasion, one of my billet mates was able to "acquire" a bottle of the Gurkha rum. I'll tell you about it a little later.

The Cambodian Dakota

A Cambodian Air Force DC3 was an occasional visitor to our pan, always bringing with it a bizarre little ritual that would never have been tolerated in the RAF. As soon as the marshaller gave the "stop" signal by holding the marshalling bats vertically above his head, the cargo door of the Dakota opened, and one or two men jumped out carrying red coloured ground-locks. They raced to the undercarriage bays where they rapidly installed the ground-locks on both undercarriage legs. Then and only then did the pilot shut the engines off. We learned that the hydraulic system on the Dakota was so leaky that it was more than likely the undercarriage would collapse if the ground-locks weren't installed while pressure from the engine-driven hydraulic pump was still available. The reverse procedure was employed for departure – engines started and then the ground-locks removed.

A Short Brothers Belfast arrived one day. It was a huge aircraft and probably the largest I had ever seen up to that point. Its mission was to carry a helicopter from Labuan to somewhere else, possibly Singapore. The chopper's rotor blades had, of course, been removed making it fit easily within the Belfast's cavernous cargo bay. Belfasts were relatively new in the RAF, so I took the opportunity to have a tour of the inside. It was nicely appointed and, in my opinion, much more luxurious than the Hercules aircraft that were also in service with the RAF. Sadly, only ten of these magnificent aircraft were ever built, all of them going into RAF service. But then, when Transport Command was merged with Bomber and Fighter Commands into the all-encompassing Strike Command, the Belfasts were disposed of, some ending up as civilian cargo haulers, ironically contracted to the very same RAF that had dumped them.

* * *

Our sergeant came into the crew room one day and asked me to take a look at a snag on a Royal Ceylon Air Force aircraft that had arrived that same day. The aircraft was a de Havilland Devon, a small, comfortable, twin piston-engine passenger plane typically used to ferry high ranking officers and VIPs around. The nature of the snag wasn't critical to the operation or safety of the Devon – it was simply that the lights in the passenger cabin didn't work. After informing me of what needed fixing, the sergeant told me to keep a note of how long I spent working on it and what materials I used. He went on to explain that the RCyAF did this kind of thing regularly; that they would arrive with snags on their aircraft that they either couldn't rectify themselves or just didn't want to go to the trouble. I agreed to keep note of the time and materials used, but also thought to myself, "What could be so difficult about fixing some lights?" I would soon find out.

I won't bore you with all the "Lecky" diagnostic stuff that starts with the obvious things, like checking the circuit fuse and then progressing from there, just that it eventually turned out to be a break in the middle of a long run of wire although the wire's insulation was intact. The puzzling thing is how it broke when held securely in the middle of a cable bundle tucked away above the passenger cabin false ceiling. I suspect the Ceylonese knew what the problem was and were hoping that the RAF would rewire the whole run, which would have been a major undertaking. And maybe I should mention that it was like an oven inside that cabin. Thankfully, in-line wire splices had been a recent addition to the RAF electrician's box of tricks. Hey, we weren't known as electro-magicians for nothing. Taking a brief respite out of the Devon sweat box, I made my way to stores where I picked up some nylon-vinyl (Nyvin) insulated 16-gauge wire and a crimping set that included some in-line splices. Back at the Devon, I chopped out a one-foot section of the old neoprene-insulated wire that included the break and spliced in an equal length of Nyvin wire, by crimping it at both ends with the in-line splices. Hey presto! The lights worked and I went off to report the time and materials to the sergeant.

And then there was the mysterious photo reconnaissance Canberra that dropped in from time to time. It deserves a chapter all to itself, which comes a little later, but first I want to describe some of what our off duty lives involved at Labuan.

Chapter 5: Off Duty Life

After a hot, sweaty day on the flight line, a cool shower back at the billets was welcome. Then it was on with the sarong and flip-flops and an evening of relaxation. The houseboy had made up the beds and swept the billet during the day and, as a last task in the late afternoon, had deployed our mosquito nets over our beds. I usually spent some time each evening, after getting back there, to write a letter to Pam. It may have been short, but we both eagerly looked forward to the daily letters. In fact, letters from home had a greater impact on everyone's morale than any other aspect of service life. When the mail arrived at the workplace, everything else stopped as each person waited with anxious anticipation to be either overjoyed at receiving a letter from home, or disappointed when that day's mail held nothing for him. There was no CHALK flight at the weekend and therefore no mail, so the Monday delivery was always eagerly anticipated.

Camp life was more communal when compared to camp life back in Britain because we were all in the same boat. Back at Waddington, for instance, the married blokes would depart for home at the end of a day shift and many of the single lads would go back to the billet, get cleaned up and change into civvies before leaving camp for an evening in the many pubs that populated the area, or to spend time with girlfriends. With no homes, pubs, or girlfriends to divert us, we were all basically "single" and, as such, hung together in a spirit of camaraderie. The NAAFI was the nearest thing we had to a pub, so many of us gathered there in the evening and consumed copious quantities of Tiger Beer. The dress code was either KD or civvy shirt and shorts. Light blue shirts that could be purchased at the little Indian shop I mentioned earlier, seemed to be the favourite fashion for most of us.

The NAAFI was a wooden building which, according to some earlier Labuan veterans, had recently replaced a tent. There was also a small Astra cinema adjacent to the NAAFI. The NAAFI wasn't too far from my billet, so it wasn't far to stagger after an evening of imbibing, although, while returning, it was prudent not to stumble over the monkey or its little home. Oh wait! I haven't mentioned the monkey! Someone had captured a small monkey and had tied it up with a collar on the end of a long chain, like a dog, in the wide, open space between rows of billets. The other end of the chain was attached to a wooden crate, set up on end, that the poor creature used for shelter. I don't know who had put it there or how long it had been in that situation, but I hoped that it was released back to the wild when the camp was finally vacated at the end of the Confrontation. As it was, many of us used to bring it bananas and other fruit from the mess to keep it fed.

My Labuan billet. The ablutions and latrines structure is on the right of the picture together with the header tank that provided the water pressure for the showers. The small wooden box in the foreground is the monkey's little "house." Apparently, the monkey wasn't home at the time.

During weekends, several of us would sit around a table in the billet to play cards. We didn't play for money, at least not in our billet, but enjoyed a couple of card games. One was Knockout Whist, and the other was Hunt the Lady, although, shame on us, we called the latter by a more vulgar name. On one memorable occasion, someone produced the bottle of the Gurkha rum that I mentioned earlier. I don't know how he acquired it and didn't really care to know. That stuff was very potent, I can tell you, and Knockout Whist lived up to its name in more ways than one. Most of us stayed in the billet and retired to our pit (translation: our bed) when the "spirit" moved us, but one of our number decided to go for a walk instead, while in a seriously inebriated state. There was a small area of jungle on the outskirts of the camp, known to most as the Ulu, into which our hero wandered and then, being suddenly overcome by an urge to take a nap, he chose to lie on an inviting patch of undergrowth, where he promptly fell asleep. The local mosquitoes must have thought that Christmas had come early, because when the unfortunate erk woke up and returned sheepishly to the billet in a more sober state, every bit of his exposed skin and much that was only covered by his thin shirt, was covered in throbbing, red lumps and bumps – evidence that a horde of opportunistic insects had enjoyed the open bar that our mate had provided for them. Judging from his blood-alcohol level, I bet there were a few mosquitoes flying very erratically after their feast that day.

Lying in bed after dark was often an interesting experience. As mentioned earlier, violent thunderstorms often passed directly overhead during the night. Brilliant flashes of lightning that seemed to last for a few seconds lit up the interior of the billet, the bright light penetrating through the wide, horizontal ventilation opening that ran around the top of the two long walls. It briefly illuminated the mosquito nets draped over our beds, which were billowing in the stiff breeze created by the whizzing ceiling fans, giving the nets the appearance of animated ghosts haunting us, and the billet an altogether eerie appearance. All of this to the accompaniment of pounding rain on our corrugated metal roof.

At other times, one of the numerous large beetles indigenous to the area would fly in through those same ventilation openings. These were nocturnal creatures about an inch in length that were an iridescent green colour if seen during daylight. We called them dung beetles, although I'm not sure that was an accurate description, although they certainly belonged to the scarab beetle family. The entrance of one of these intruders was very noticeable by the raspy sound made by its flight. We all lay in silence, waiting for the inevitable to happen. And sooner or later, it did – the unfortunate critter would make contact with one of the whizzing ceiling fans and with a loud "b'doyng!" would ricochet off the fan in some random direction, usually to land on one someone's mosquito net. Sometimes, its next destination was beetle heaven, but they were tough, heavily armoured little bastards, and could often survive the experience, ending up clinging to the material of the net by little hooks on their rear legs. Those that survived eventually found their own way out or were removed in the morning by the house boy.

When all had gone quiet in the billet, being young men separated by many miles and many months from wives and girlfriends, some, and probably all at some time or another, experienced what could be charitably referred to as 'nocturnal emissions' or, let's say, taking matters in hand, or finding a handy remedy for the problem. Do I need to go on, or do you get the idea? Anyway, this usually happened, mostly quietly, in the dead of night and with no one else supposedly being aware. Enter the house boy! While making our beds, or during the weekly sheet change, he would see evidence of this activity and, when the unfortunate airman entered the billet at lunchtime, the house boy would loudly exclaim "Wanker, wanker!" much to that individual's embarrassment.

Some lads found other ways to relieve their sexual stress, such as consorting with the professional virgins in Victoria, the island's main town. These ladies haunted the bars, and it was impossible to sit in a bar without being accosted by one of them. They wouldn't go away and at the very least, pestered you to buy them a drink, but also offered other more intimate services, should one wish to take advantage of them. They were mostly an ugly lot – one was known notoriously by the nickname "Fort Knox" by all and sundry, although she may have been one of the *Mama Sans,* one in each bar, who oversaw the ladies and directed them to their targets, namely us. But her nickname was earned because of her mouthful of gold teeth that must have cost her a small fortune – possibly an investment of her earnings.

In all honesty, I never fell for the temptation of the "other services" but did buy them drinks – you couldn't avoid doing so, because they would continue to pester you until you did. When you eventually agreed to buy the drink, the server would bring the woman a small glass of coloured liquid that was added to your tab at a highly inflated price. But getting back to those other services, the only way I could imagine anyone accepting the offer would be if he were stone drunk because those women were so unattractive. However, one lad in my billet, who got married just before being posted to Labuan, succumbed on at least one occasion. Then, shortly before the end of his one-year tour, he discovered that he had contracted a sexually transmitted disease. I don't remember if it was gonorrhoea or syphilis, but he was in a state of panic about getting it cured. With little time left before his repatriation, the chances of that were slim. I often wonder what happened to him. Did he get cured, or if not, how did he explain the predicament to his bride.

I did have one nasty, scary experience in a Victoria bar. Several of us from the squadron were there for a communal night out on the town. Several tables had been placed together, end to end, making one long table that we all sat around. Of course, we were quickly joined by "the girls" who were making the usual requests for us to buy them drinks; all of this presided over by the *Mama San.* A teenage girl, probably about 14 or 15, was bringing the drinks around, Tiger beer for the lads and coloured water for our "hostesses." I had finished the latest bottle I'd been drinking and wanted another when the little waitress came nearby to bring someone else's drink, so I reached out and touched her arm to get her attention. Her reaction was as though she had received an electric shock – I can think of no better way to describe it. She jumped back a few feet and then grabbed an empty bottle off her tray and holding it by the neck, smashed the bottom part down on the edge of a table. Then, in the same fluid movement, she pointed the resulting jagged end towards my face. At the same time, she glared at me with undisguised anger and hatred. I backed off very quickly and held both hands up, palms facing her to show that I meant her no harm. At the same time, the *Mama San* jumped into action and came quickly around to the girl to drag her back, away from me. I tried to say I was sorry and hadn't meant any harm because she had apparently taken my touch on her arm to mean something else, but she continued to glare while the *Mama San* disarmed her and hustled her out through a doorway and out of the bar. I looked around, because everything had gone noticeably quiet, and saw that all the others were staring at me with open mouths. Just then, somebody exclaimed, "Fuck me!" in a tone of voice that registered his and everyone else's utter surprise at what had just occurred. That broke the spell because everyone then began talking excitedly about the incident. Evidently, the young waitress didn't want to graduate to become one of "the girls" and probably despised the whole thing but was having to assist in the sordid business for reasons at which we can only guess. We stayed there in the bar and continued our beer session, but yours truly felt very shaken up for the rest of the evening and I was glad when we all called it a day and headed back to camp.

One of our number was a bit luckier in having his needs satisfied than the rest of us. He was a fine looking, unmarried young man of average build and of the clean-cut variety that mothers wish their daughters would bring home to dinner instead of the scuzzy types that they usually do bring. Altar boy material if ever I saw it. His name escapes me now, so let's just call him Michael. At the same time, I need to explain that there were two WVS women assigned to the camp, both of whom resided in a nice house on the outskirts of the camp. WVS stands for Women's Voluntary Service; they wore green, buttoned-up the front dresses and helped to organize recreational activities for the troops, like barbecues on the beach amongst other things. One of them, a slight woman, appeared to be in her sixties and behaved appropriately for her age. The other one, I would guess, was in her late forties or early fifties. She was a tall, sturdily built woman who spoke with a posh, cut-glass accent. She also had features that fitted in well with the well-to-do horsey set, having prominent, protruding front teeth and a long, otherwise unremarkable face. For that reason, she was known behind her back as "The Horse." In short, she was no oil painting. However, as the saying goes, 'In the land of the blind, the one-eyed man is king' – she, being one of the two only British women on a remote RAF camp populated by a bunch of randy young men, had her pick of who to consort with. Michael apparently met her requirements and had become what would be known in later decades as her toy-boy. He rarely spent nights in the billet and when anyone tried to pull his leg about his relationship with The Horse, he just responded with a satisfied smirk – a *very* satisfied smirk.

On one occasion, the same Michael was the source of a flurry of excitement and activity tinged with panic that had nothing to do directly with The Horse. There was a small boat pulled up on the gently sloping, palm tree fringed beach that we used for the barbecues. The little boat was the kind used by army types in that era to infiltrate beaches and rivers. It was noticeably light weight; probably made of aluminium and dark green in colour and had apparently been "acquired" for recreational purposes. Michael was in the habit of using it to paddle out into the strait that separated the island of Labuan from the Borneo mainland, which was roughly five miles across at its narrowest point, although he usually kept close to shore. Late one afternoon, he paddled off by himself and was somewhere out there when a heavy tropical storm descended on the area. Visibility was reduced to near zero by the torrential downpour that fell from the dark thunderclouds. When it eventually passed through, Michael was nowhere to be seen. I don't know who raised the alarm, but possibly it was The Horse. A frantic call was made to one of the helicopter squadrons on the Labuan at that time, either 110 or 103 squadron. A chopper was launched soon after to search for the little boat, hopefully with Michael still safely inside. But because it was late – remember, the sun sets at around 6 pm in that part of the world – the light was fading fast, so the helicopter crew had to call off the search. At dawn the next morning, a helicopter was again launched and eventually the crew spotted the boat pulled up on a mainland beach with Michael asleep inside. The helicopter landed and found him to be suffering from several insect bites, because he was clad only in swimming trunks, but otherwise unharmed. He was taken on board the chopper, to which the boat was secured by a long line, they then flew back to the Labuan at low level, towing the boat behind them and all ended well.

Although I never used the boat, swimming was my favourite pastime, taking advantage of our proximity to beaches and the relative coolness of the ocean around Labuan. Being in the water was a nice way to cool off and escape from the heat, although it was only possible at the weekends, not being practical during the working week because it got dark so early. There was a small cove adjacent to the camp that was reached by a flight of wooden stairs that had been installed sometime previously. It was fairly safe to swim there, but we were cautioned to be aware of Lionfish that appeared to be feathery and soft, but the long "feathers" concealed very sharp, poisonous barbs that could inflict severe pain and, in some cases, could even be deadly. The other thing we were advised to beware of was sea snakes, which were also deadly venomous.

It so happened that the small NAAFI shop on the camp sold facemasks, snorkels, and flippers, all of good quality. The flippers were the kind that fitted like a shoe and were long and strong. I invested in a set of this swimming equipment, and it made all the difference to the experience. Not only was the facemask a good way to see what was in my vicinity under the water, not that I ever saw a Lionfish, but on one occasion, while I was a few feet below the surface, I suddenly became aware of a wriggling shape above me that I took to be a snake. It didn't bother me, but swam over me, on the surface.

Usually, there were also other swimmers in the water, but one time I was down there alone. Perhaps it wasn't a good idea to go into the water with no one else there, but I did, young and foolish as I was. While swimming around, a few feet under again, this time I became aware of some shapes hanging about above me. Looking up, I saw two skinny-looking fish, each about maybe two feet long, circling above me. My immediate thought was barracudas, so with powerful strokes of my flippers I beat it to hell out of the water. It turned out that they were harmless (to humans anyway) trumpetfish that like to hang around larger non-predatory fish and turtles as a hunting strategy. Maybe I looked like a big fish to them and that's why they were circling me.

While the cove was convenient, there weren't too many fish there. A better place was a pier in Victoria that was owned or used by Shell Oil and was therefore known as the Shell pier. Swimming around it was like swimming in a giant aquarium. There were countless colourful tropical fish of the size that would have made them suitable for a home aquarium. Some were striped and had a shape that somehow brings the name angelfish to mind, others were bright, solidly coloured, while many were speckled. It was fun swimming amongst them around and under the pier. A large school of small, silvery, iridescent fishes always seemed to stay under the pier, turning all at the same time as though someone was controlling them, their silvery bodies flashing with reflected light as they turned. To swim towards them with the intention of bumping into some of them was impossible because they just parted like a silver curtain leaving just sufficient room for me to pass through the school without coming into contact with any of them. All the while, hundreds of dark little fisheyes kept a close watch on me so that the school could anticipate any change in my direction. After I passed through it, the "curtain" closed behind me again as though my passage had never happened. I spent many hours, as did many of my Labuan mates, snorkelling under the Shell pier like a would-be Jacques Cousteau.

Chapter 6: Sheep-Dip?

Meanwhile, back on the flight line, one of our regular transiting visitors was a mysterious-looking Canberra PR7. It was painted matte all over, jungle camouflage on top and matte black on the underside. It also had very few markings, and those that it did have were quite subdued. I don't recall seeing any squadron identification. The matte black underbelly was punctuated by a few flat, optical glass panels through which reconnaissance photographs would be taken, which was understandable since the "PR" designation stands for "Photo Reconnaissance." We were cautioned never to mention the aircraft by its 'Canberra' name, but to always refer to it as a "twin jet."

When the pilot and navigator disembarked and were driven off to the officers' mess, the assigned ground crew refuelled the aircraft, and kept its interior cool by setting a locally made sunshade of canvas on a bamboo frame over the canopy bubble, as well as inserting a large flexible duct that pumped chilled air into the crew compartment. The flight crew returned quite some time later, presumably after a meal in the mess and, appreciative of the nice cool interior, strapped in, started up and took off. The Canberra – er, sorry, twin jet – would then return the following day, whereupon the same routine would be repeated before it took off again, this time on its way back to wherever it came from.

On one occasion, having been detailed to be a member of the turn-round ground crew, I recognized the Canberra pilot of this particular sortie as a former flying instructor at Cranwell, where we had both been stationed a few years earlier. I even remembered his name, Flt. Lt. N***, although he was now a Squadron Leader according to the rank insignia on his flight suit epaulettes. He in turn remembered me, or at least recognized my face, as one of the ground crew that had often helped him and his trainee pilots strap into a Vampire T11 when he was instructing Cranwell cadets in the art of flying. So, while he waited for transport to the mess, we had a brief chat, recalling our time at the RAF College. During the conversation, I casually asked him what the Canberra was going to be photographing. He replied, equally casually, that they would be taking pictures of the Indonesian – Malaysian border on the Borneo mainland. His answer satisfied my idle curiosity, so I just assumed that they would be landing at RAF Kuching on the Borneo mainland and would spend the night there before making the return trip, presumably to RAF Tengah in Singapore, which was home to a Canberra PR7 squadron – number 81 Squadron, to be precise. It didn't really cross my mind at the time as to why it would be necessary for the aircraft to land and refuel at Labuan if it had been to another nearby station, Kuching perhaps, on the Borneo mainland. Meanwhile, life continued as normal, and I just put the episode to the back of my mind with the other memories of my time at Labuan, only to have it resurface, rather unexpectedly, several years later.

* * *

It was twenty-two years later when, as a civilian engineer working in America, I was engaged in a project with a Unocal oil company engineer and he and I got talking about our backgrounds. When I mentioned that I had been in the RAF back in the fifties and sixties, he quickly responded that he had been in the USAF around that same time. During the Vietnam War, he said that he had been involved in some clandestine work with the CIA in neighbouring Laos. It seems that he had been "sheep-dipped," to use the American military's expression for someone plucked out of normal service life and secretly sent to work for the "spooks." The CIA, he went on to tell me, operated its own private airline known as "Air America" (something I found out later to be true) that had civilian markings but was used to support many kinds of covert operations in Laos, Cambodia, and Thailand, as well as Vietnam. One of its activities was monitoring the movements of the Vietcong along the so-called Ho Chi Minh Trail in Laos. During a few drinks after our engineering meeting, he regaled me with story after story about the things his Air America group got up to during those days, portraying them as some kind of supermen. Apparently, they were good at everything, except photo reconnaissance. "That's where the RAF came in," he said, "and you guys did a super job for us."

This took me a bit by surprise. "I don't think it was the RAF – Britain wasn't involved in the Vietnam War," I said, adding "It was probably the Australian Air Force. They were in the Vietnam War."

"No, it was definitely the RAF," he replied. "A RAF photo reconnaissance Canberra frequently landed at our airfield in the middle of the night, after photographing the Ho Chi Minh Trail." (He pronounced it Can-BERR-a with the emphasis on the second syllable, as the Americans typically do). "We unloaded the films from the cameras as the Can-BERR-a was being refuelled and then it took off again, while it was still dark, and left the area. We just didn't have anything at that time that could do the job as good."

For a few moments, I just couldn't believe what he was telling me, but then the memory of the "twinjet" that occasionally passed through Labuan, supposedly on the way to photograph the Indonesian-Malaysian border came to mind. "Holy shit!" I exclaimed, more to myself than to my informant, "That's where it was going!"

Later, thinking about what I had been told and piecing it together with what I had witnessed at Labuan, it seemed to explain why the mysterious Canberra left Labuan one day and didn't return until the next. If what I suspected was true, then it was more likely that the Canberra was refuelled in Vietnam or Laos by the Air America ground crew, instead of our people at Kuching. Then there would have been the need for another refuelling stop and a break for the flight crew before it completed the final leg back to Tengah – at least I assumed it was Tengah. But I was content to leave it there in the knowledge that possibly the British government's public denial that we were involved in the Vietnam War was not all honest and above board. But then, what's new? Just like when Harold Macmillan assured the public that we weren't involved in the Cuban Missile Crisis, despite the fact that the entire V-bomber force at that time was nuked up to the teeth and sitting at 15 minutes readiness to scramble for a one-way trip to the USSR. And I knew *that* was a bald-faced lie, having been one of those that spent four days stationed on the Operational Readiness Platform (ORP) at the end of a runway where four nuclear armed Vulcans were just waiting for the word to scramble – word which thankfully never came.

Now, more than fifty years later, wanting to include the story in this book, I set about doing some research in an effort to get my facts straight, but only with mixed success as it happened. First of all, to which squadron did the Canberra belong? It wasn't difficult to discover that 81 Squadron, based at Tengah, and equipped with Canberra PR7 aircraft, was the only photo reconnaissance squadron in the Far East Air Force. Obviously, that's where my Canberra had originated, or so it seemed and, as luck would have it, I came across an active website operated by the Tengah veterans of that very squadron. When I contacted the webmaster, he was intrigued by the story, but said that he hadn't been on the squadron at that time and passed my query on to a former navigator from the relevant time period.

The navigator, named Hally Hardie, quickly poured cold water on my "Tengah" theory by explaining that all Canberra aircraft on 81 squadron were painted in standard Far East livery of grey and green on the upper half and grey underneath, all in gloss finish, not matte. He also questioned the logic of flying from Tengah to Labuan and then to Vietnam – why not fly directly from Tengah, since it was just as much within range of Vietnam as Labuan?

Also, to quote him verbatim, *"What I am sure of is that the photo technology of the time, as practiced by the RAF, could not have returned any useful imagery from night photo at any level even with the 5" photo flares or alternative 1.75" cartridges as then used. However, this does not preclude the use of superior technology provided by the Yanks, or even IR linescan, the former could have used the standard camera bays, but the latter would almost certainly have been via an exterior pod - maybe in the bomb bay - due to its size."*

Despite his observation about the lack of RAF night-time photographic reconnaissance, Hally and I continued to correspond for quite some time, during which we explored other possibilities. At first, he theorized that the aircraft my informant had seen was the American built version of the Canberra, known as the B57. These had, in fact, been used in Vietnam for photo reconnaissance, but the former USAF/CIA guy had been emphatic that the aircraft he and his colleagues turned round was a Royal Air Force Canberra with an RAF crew. One other possibility I thought of was the RAAF base at Darwin on the tip of Australia's Northern Territory. It was within range of Labuan and was more of a direct route to Vietnam than routing through Singapore, but I wasn't sure how to pursue that line of enquiry and so put it on one side. Instead, we considered other origination points for the mystery craft.

The next nearest Canberra PR squadrons were based in Malta and Cyprus. So, what if the Canberra flew from one of those and refuelled at Gan? Hally was a bit sceptical of that theory, implying that the flying distance from Gan to Labuan was impractical. He said that when his Canberra crew flew from the Mediterranean to Singapore, they refuelled at Colombo in Ceylon. Well, that route would work, but it still didn't confirm the origin of the Canberra. Had it come from somewhere in the Mediterranean or somewhere further afield? Searching the Internet for any other information, I came across the following, "*While doing some research on the web a few months ago I was surprised to find a news article (from a Cypriot newspaper I think) where the locals were worried that a night-stopping Canberra at Akrotiri could be used to spy on the host nation.*" That would imply Germany as a possible point of origin, or maybe it came from the UK.

There was a legitimate reason to fly to Labuan because the RAF had every reason to be there, namely The Confrontation, where there were fewer prying eyes and ears to see or overhear its arrival and departure. This was perhaps borne out by the caution given to all of us on 209 Squadron to refer to the Canberra only as a twinjet. Once at Labuan, the route to Vietnam would be mostly across open ocean, which would make it less likely to be seen. Besides, that would also have been its route from Labuan to another legitimate destination - Hong Kong, during which a last-minute change of course could take the Canberra, at high altitude, over the narrow part of Vietnam and into Laotian airspace.

Hally suggested that I try to obtain some information from the MOD by using the Freedom of Information Act. It was a good idea, so I gave it a try, but after a few weeks, received a response telling me that it was too long ago to be in the MOD records and suggested that I try the National Archives. So, I tried that too, but it's not a case of asking, instead it means entering a search subject and then looking through the titles of a long list of catalogues that remotely relate to the subject. It was like looking for a needle in a haystack, so at that point I gave up.

And so, to summarize; on several occasions, a Canberra PR7 aircraft transited through RAF Labuan on its way to an unknown destination and didn't return until the next day. It may have been the same aircraft each time, but it also might have been one of a few that were similar in appearance, although it now seems clear that a Canberra painted in a matte colour scheme was a rarity, so it may very well have been the same one each time.

The destination must have been a considerable distance away, as was its origin, because not only was refuelling necessary each time it landed, but the pilot and navigator were hungry both times and needed a meal and a break, suggesting that they had flown a long sortie prior to landing. I know this for certain because I was there and was involved in the turn-rounds. Its destination after the first turn-round is a matter of speculation. Or it could be considered circumstantial evidence when my ex-USAF informant's story is combined with my observation of its arrivals and departures at Labuan, making the Vietnam (or Laos) destination fit in with the Canberra's departure and subsequent return the next day, after an apparently lengthy flight.

As for its origin and routes – all of that is pure speculation based on "straws in the wind," but I have finally settled on the theory that the PR7 began its journey from Australia, possibly the Darwin base, which is within range of Labuan, and returned there afterwards. At that time, the Aussies were involved in the Vietnam war, but didn't have an operational photo reconnaissance squadron. Number 87 squadron, their only one, had been disbanded in 1953. And although the RAAF did have Canberra bombers, it didn't have any PR7 Canberra aircraft or crews trained to operate them. Therefore, it's possible that one or more RAF PR7s and flight crews were seconded to the RAAF to provide needed and legitimate intelligence, which was also shared with the CIA in the form of Air America. But understandably, the RAF involvement would have been kept secret. Finally, it can be seen, by looking at the world map, that a straight line drawn between Darwin in Australia's Northern Territory and Vietnam passes directly over Borneo. Also, that the Labuan's location is approximately halfway between the two, making it an ideal refuelling stop for such an operation.

And there I must leave it, in the absence of any concrete evidence, but perhaps someone who reads this may have a little more light to throw on the subject.

Chapter 7: Changi

In late November of 1966, FEAF HQ finally received the news, possibly delivered by carrier pigeon, that the *Konfrontasi* with Indonesia had been brought to a satisfactory conclusion and that a peace agreement had been signed four months earlier. Shortly afterwards, we members of the squadron were informed that the detachment was going to be run down. Consequently, those of our number who had served more than 6 months of their tour would be immediately repatriated and credited with a full tour. On the other hand, those with less than 6 months of service, which included me, would have their tour converted to a full 30 months and be transferred to one of the stations in Singapore. Also, those of us who were married would now be able to have our wives and children join us at the new station. I didn't have any children but was overjoyed that Pam would now be able to be with me in Singapore. Forms were then promptly distributed so that we could make formal application to have our loved ones brought out from the U.K.

On the 12th of December, I boarded the 48 Squadron CHALK Hastings for the bone-jarring flight back to Changi, having kept the vow I had made to myself when I first arrived that the only time I would ever take a flight from Labuan was the one on which I would begin my homeward-bound journey. Although it wasn't technically on my way home, it was the next best thing because Pam and I would be back together again and the old saying that goes — Home is where the Heart is. So far, so good, but it would take another month for all the arrangements to be made before she could fly out to Singapore. Meanwhile, it meant we would be spending Christmas apart, but it was a small price to pay.

During the Changi "Arrivals" process, I learned that my internal posting was to the Electronics Squadron, but meanwhile, I was back in the Changi transit billet, which now seemed quite civilized after having spent time in its counterpart at Labuan, but I knew I wouldn't be there for long. Incidentally, I heard from fellow airman Ian Duckham, who was in Communications and therefore one of the last to leave Labuan. He told me that, with the rundown of the camp, he and his few remaining colleagues were moved into the former Sergeants Mess, where they had air conditioning together with hot and cold running water. They must have thought they had died and gone to Heaven.

When I had originally arrived at Changi, prior to continuing on to Labuan, it had been very obvious how tan everyone appeared compared to the paleness of those of us who had just arrived from the U.K. Now things appeared decidedly different. My time on the flight line at Labuan, stripped off to the waist, had resulted in a deep tan, so now I noticed how pale the Changi personnel were in comparison. The deepness would eventually fade, and I would acquire a Singapore tan, but for that short time, it was noticeable not just to me, but to others.

The Electronics Squadron turned out to be a building not far off the Changi Road on the street that led towards the airfield and the hangars. The centrally located entrance to the building opened to a corridor that went off in both directions, left and right. Offices for the various engineering officers and the admin staff, arrayed along the outside wall, opened off this corridor. One large room served as a break room in which a young Chinese brother and sister, in their twenties I would guess, operated a snack bar that served hot and cold food. It provided a good income for them, but they had to put up with a lot of verbal abuse from some of my fellow airmen and, understandably, they made it plain that they didn't like any of us.

A doorway set centrally on the inside wall of the corridor led to a large room in the interior of the building that was partitioned off in an open plan type of arrangement and which housed second line servicing personnel and equipment of all the electrical and electronic trades. A central aisle led from the door towards the rear of the building, the Electrical Section being the first section on the right and the Instruments Section occupied the opposite side, the two together jointly referred to as the E&I Section. The Radio and Radar Sections were located in the rear half of the room.

I wasn't too unhappy about being in this environment, the building was air-conditioned after all, which was a boon in the hot and humid Singapore climate, and it was mostly an 8 am to 5 pm job. The downside however was that it removed me from working directly on aircraft – at least for most of the time, although I did get some opportunities later on. But at last, I could finally wear the tailored KD that I had bought in Changi Village when I first arrived, while waiting for the flight to Labuan, since most others on the station were wearing it.

When I reported to the Electronics Squadron Admin Office, blue arrivals card in hand, I was given the details of which barrack block to move into. That's where I would have to lay my head until Pam joined me, and then I could "live out." Next, I was introduced to the Electrical Officer and the Squadron Warrant Officer. After welcoming me and asking a few details about my service history, the W.O. took me to the Electrical Section and introduced me to Sergeant Jackson-Smith, the SNCO in charge of the Electrical Section, to whom I would be reporting directly, and left me with him.

Sergeant Jackson-Smith was a pleasant man who was quite easy to get along with. On our first meeting, he was interested in my prior experience working in the Electronics Centre at Scampton and particularly in my experience testing alternators there, so I wasn't surprised when he said he would put me in charge of the Changi generator and alternator testing.

The day passed quickly as I familiarized myself with the section and met the other corporals and airmen who worked there. There was a medium-sized room off to the side of the main area where the generator test rig was located. The rig itself was the current standard model that I was familiar with from Scampton, but unlike Scampton, the generators were not stripped down and serviced by airmen. Instead, a small number of local men were employed to do that particular dirty job. Two that I remember were both mature men –

one was a Chinese named Lee and the other was a Malay named Saad. The latter lived in the nearby Kampong Changi and possibly Lee did as well, although I don't know that for sure, but both were friendly and easy to get along with, unlike the break-room brother and sister. The area where they did the servicing was an annex to the main building. It wasn't air-conditioned, but the two men seemed happy enough to be working in that environment.

After work, my next job was moving from the transit billet to the squadron barrack block. Like most buildings on the domestic site, it had been built in the 1930s when it was an army base and before it became an RAF base after the Second World War. It could be best described as colonial style, like many of the older buildings in Singapore. It was a three-storey, white painted concrete structure, my billet being on the middle floor. The billet itself was a large, high-ceilinged room, with the obligatory ceiling fans rotating at full speed all day and night and was accessed from a wide balcony that ran parallel to it on the outer side of the building. Another billet and balcony occupied the opposite side of the floor in a mirror image, so the only ventilation came from doors and windows on the wall adjacent to the balcony.

Out on the balcony, rows of tiny ants marched along the lower edge of the openings and inside, I noticed, the legs of the beds were set in small metal dishes, some of which contained liquid. The liquid turned out to be oil that was used as an impassable barrier for the ants, which would otherwise invade a person's bed. One thing also became very obvious – there were no mosquito nets. Changi employed a crew of local men as fumigators who went around the camp with portable fogging machines that were used in mosquito breeding areas in an effort to keep the pests down. And it was fairly successful, although that's not to say that there weren't any around – a few of the little buggers always seemed to be able to evade the fogging machine. But as Singapore was considered to be a non-malaria area, mosquito nets weren't necessary for protection while sleeping and therefore were not provided by the bedding store.

Since the barrack block was going to be my home for only the next three and a half weeks, the question of where Pam and I would live when she arrived was much on my mind. So, I visited the Families Accommodation Flight to get some advice. Young airmen like me didn't have enough "points" to qualify for a married quarter on the camp, so I needed to explore the alternatives, of which there weren't many. From my visit to Families and conversations with other married people in the E&I Section, it soon became obvious that the monopoly for privately rented married accommodation was held by several grocery shops in the surrounding area. The conventional wisdom was that when you rented a house from one of these grocers, you were expected to purchase your groceries from them. Housing was supposedly scarce, according to the Families people, so the grocers had tenants by the short and curlies. As it happened, this advice turned out to be untrue because things had changed recently. With the beginnings of the withdrawal of British and Commonwealth Forces following the end of Confrontation, there were fewer potential tenants for the grocers to exploit. I didn't quite know that at the time, but it soon became obvious.

On the 19th of December 1966, just one week after I had arrived at Changi, the long-anticipated telegram arrived containing the simple message, "COMING 5TH JANUARY. LOVE PAM." She would actually leave her parents' home in Lincoln on Wednesday the 4th, travel to London and stay overnight in a Heathrow airport hotel, ready to board the British Eagle flight on Thursday, arriving in Singapore on Friday, January 6th, 1967. Although it seemed an age at the time, things had moved really fast from the time that I had applied for her to join me. The next two weeks would drag, especially since we would miss being together for Christmas, meanwhile I was living the single life.

There wasn't a NAAFI canteen on the camp although there was NAAFI shop. However, there was a Corporals' Club, but it wasn't used very much by the living-in corporals, including yours truly, because everyone seemed to patronise the Malcolm Club where appetising food was available for reasonable prices. Also, nearby Changi Village was a good destination for food and drinks. The village consisted of more than bars, though. It was a shopping Mecca for all manner of cameras, electronic luxury goods, bespoke tailors, as well as household goods. One of the things I needed badly, having just come from Labuan, was a haircut, and there were a few barbers' shops in Changi Village. I picked one and entered it and was soon seated in a barber's chair. If I was expecting the usual "short back and sides" typical of UK barbers, I was in for quite a big surprise. First, the Chinese barber slapped a steaming hot towel over my face. It was a momentary shock at first, but welcome when he let it sit for a short while and then used it to wipe my sweaty face. He then proceeded to cut my hair, all the while chatting to his fellow barbers in Chinese. When he had finished the haircutting, there was another surprise in store – he suddenly began massaging my scalp and then my shoulders, at times doing rapid mini karate chops along the tops of my shoulders and doing something with cupped hands just below the back of my neck. I enjoyed all of it, although it was unusual. It turned out that this procedure was standard with all the Singapore barbers and something that I wished the "back-home" barbers would perform.

Now that I would be wearing non-RAF issue KD, I needed to buy some more, and Changi village was the place to get it. This time, I shopped around because there was more than one tailor shop in the village. Previously, I was a bit "green" when it came to making purchases in Singapore and had paid the asking price, just as people normally did back home. But now that I'd been in the Far East for a little while, the concept of bargaining had taken root. After shopping around for a while, it became obvious that I had paid too much for that first set of KD, even though it seemed cheap at the time, so after some bargaining, I acquired two more sets complete with white corporal stripes on the arms.

Speaking of bargaining, there was an art to using it to get a fair price, but it was a learned skill gained mostly by learning from the lads who had been there for some time and by personal experience. The worst thing a potential buyer could do in Singapore, and probably anywhere else in the Far East, was to walk into a shop and buy an expensive item, let's say a camera, on impulse. That was a sure way to get fleeced because those shops and merchants weren't like those back in Britain, where prices were fixed, and it was the standard thing to just pay that fixed price. In Singapore, the most important thing to do was decide what you wanted to acquire before going shopping for it – brand name and the model or style, and then do some research to discover its list price. That was a little more challenging in those pre-Internet days, but it could be done. Most high-end items, such as cameras or stereo equipment, were imported from Japan by the local agent for that brand. Once you found the agent, it was possible to find out the list price because that's the price the agent would quote. You didn't purchase the item from that source, of course, but with the information, the next thing to do was to go to a shop that sold it. Most of the time, that would be in Changi village, where the merchants were used to RAF types and had a higher volume of turnover than shops in Singapore proper, therefore a better price could be negotiated. Knowing the list price, it was then a good rule of thumb to ask the merchant how much to buy the item. Chances were that it would be close to the list price, but a little less. Often, the merchant or his employee would utter phrases such as, "For you, John, I give a special price," and then knock a few dollars off. But the trick was to counteroffer with a figure that was half the list price and watch for the reaction. Usually, it was like throwing ice water on the person because your offer cut deeply into the profit margin or wiped it out entirely. From there, he would counter with something less than the price he first quoted, but still much higher than you wanted to pay. The object was to try to get a price that was around ten or twenty percent above your original half-list price offer. Typically, a back and forth between the two parties would then ensue, each offer whittling down the difference between his offer and yours until he would go no further, which ideally was around the price you wanted to pay. If you couldn't get there, then it was time to resort to the final ploy, which was to turn around and start to walk out of the shop. At that point, you had to be prepared to keep walking, but typically, the merchant would call you back and settle for the price you offered, or close to it.

    Now, here's where I need to contradict something I mentioned earlier – that prices in Britain were fixed and non-negotiable. Not really! The same tactics, I discovered, could also be used back home in certain situations, mostly when it came to buying expensive items such as furniture or cars. But more about that later.

* * *

During the brief period of living the single life, some people from my past life crossed my path. There was Leon, who I served with on the Vampire flight line at Cranwell. He invited me home for dinner and to meet his wife and children – a gesture of hospitality that was enjoyed. Then there was Anna. She had been a fellow student at my childhood school in Coleraine – we had even lived on the same street at that time. We accidentally met while we were both waiting at a bus stop on Changi Road after my visit to Leon's house. I didn't realize who she was until I heard her Coleraine accent when she began talking to someone else. Then, when I looked at her face more closely, I then realized who she was. "Anna O'B****," I exclaimed. She, in turn, recognized me at that moment. We caught up on our joint histories during the years that had passed since we both attended St. Malachy's School. She was now married to a Navy man – an aircraft technician in the Fleet Air Arm and stationed in Singapore. Her brother had married one of my cousins, although I wasn't aware of that nugget of family history until she told me. So, we were actually related by marriage. Anna gave me the address of the happy couple, who were then living in Scunthorpe, in the off chance that I might be able to visit them after being repatriated, which I did manage to do.

Last, but not least was Barry Goodall, a fellow electrician and friend from Waddington, who was now working on 205 Shackleton Squadron. I don't actually remember meeting Barry at Changi, so the reader might think it strange why I would mention him. The reason is indeed strange and begs an explanation, so here goes. When putting together my previous book, *Vulcan on the Line*, I included a photo from my personal collection, which showed a group of lads in a bar setting that was obviously in a tropical country, judging from how everyone was dressed. Two of those lads were Barry Goodall and me. Because Barry had served with me on Vulcans at Waddington, I assumed the photo had been taken at one of the sleazy bars in "The Gut" in Valletta, Malta, where we had been on an exercise (Malta, not the Gut), so had included it in that chapter. Then, shortly after publishing *Vulcan on the Line*, I received an email from reader David Marinholz, which reads as follows:

> "Hi Brian, Just read and enjoyed your book ...however, I'd got two thirds through when I turned the page and I found myself looking at.......myself! During the time in the book you wrote about Luqa, there is a photo with the caption 'A few of us lads enjoying some liquid etc'. This photo depicts me sat in middle, Terry Treadgold to my left, and of course my partner in crime Barry Goodall. I racked my brain trying to fathom out the venue. It couldn't have been the Malcolm Club in Changi because there was a tablecloth on the table! Can't be Labuan cos there were no walls in the camp bar, so it can only be 205's favourite watering hole - The Milly Bar in Changi village!! So what I am trying to say is that I never went to Malta and this photo is 205 (Squadron) oriented."

I only vaguely recall meeting Barry at Changi, but the evidence was right there in my own photo album and reinforced by David's final sentence, saying that he had never been to Malta. The photographer is also a person of mystery but may have been a bar hostess who was asked to take it. As for how it came into my possession – I can only claim Tiger beer induced memory loss because I'm sure we quaffed a few that day, especially being in the company of Barry Goodall. Anyway, the photo was removed from subsequent copies of *Vulcan on the Line,* but is reproduced here, where it rightfully belongs.

***

    Christmas Day fell on a Sunday that year and service life relaxed during the week leading up to it. The squadrons and many of the sections; Station Workshops, Aircraft Servicing Flight (ASF) amongst others, got into the holiday mood by setting up "bars," all of them trying to outdo the others in creativity. It was fun to go around the station visiting the various bars and having a beer at some. One that I remember featured a Spitting Cobra in a cage. Visitors were warned not to get too close to it because it literally spat venom for quite a distance and aimed for the eyes. It was an interesting exhibit even if having to give it a wide berth.

    On Christmas Day, I went to the Airmen's' Mess for the traditional Christmas Dinner where we lower ranks were waited on by officers and senior NCOs. Afterwards, the word was that the Malcolm Club would be staging a talent contest, so I headed over there. Many of the other attendees were Navy people and it was they who were organizing the contest. Some sang songs that were enjoyable, others sang songs and were booed off-stage, poor sods. There were two acts that I remember most clearly. One was a tall matelot who did a parody striptease. I could see two of the WVS women watching and smiling as he went through his routine, which seemed as though it wasn't his first time doing it. The routine was funny and had us all laughing as he mimicked the seductive actions of a female striptease artiste. Everyone was probably wondering how far he would go, at least I was and probably so were the WVS ladies. Finally, he got to the point where he was wearing only his underwear and, in one quick movement, he turned around so that his back was to the audience, reached behind and pulled down the waistband of his underpants, but only as far as it took to reveal his bare buttocks where a big pair of wide-open eyes stared back at us, one boldly tattooed on each cheek. The club resounded with howls of laughter and a long, long round of applause. Maybe, with being in the Navy, he needed to have those eyes there!

The other act that comes to mind was performed by another sailor. This one, who had a full set of reddish whiskers, came out on the floor with a glass of what appeared to be whisky in one hand. When he had everyone's attention, he raised the glass to his lips and took a mouthful of the liquid but didn't swallow it. He then produced a cigarette lighter which he held a short distance in front of his mouth and flicked it to produce a flame. With cheeks bulging, he forcefully blew the contents of his mouth out towards the flickering lighter flame. In an instant, the cloud of whisky-saturated vapour being expelled from his pursed lips caught alight and became a long, expanding tongue of flame, only to extinguish as quickly as it had caught alight. The bearded sailor took another gulp of whisky and once again performed his human blowlamp act. One more time – it was the last gulp – he expelled it from his lips, but this time something didn't go the way it was supposed to. His beard caught alight. He didn't seem to notice at first, but a couple of audience members sitting nearest to him jumped up and ran towards him. By this time, he was aware of the problem and began beating at his lower face with his hands, but not having much success in putting the flames out. The two men grabbed hold of him and one, who had been holding a part full glass of beer, tossed the drink onto the unfortunate man's face, while the other beat out the flame where the liquid hadn't landed. I think the two of them got to him in enough time to prevent any serious burns from damaging his face, but it was a damned near thing.

Christmas Day was enjoyable, but Changi was like a ghost town for the next few days because everyone was off for the holiday, and I felt miserable being on my own at such a "together" time of the year. The bars in Changi village offered some solace, so I spent quite a bit of time visiting them, taking the "Tiger" by the tail, so to speak, while moping that it would take another two weeks before Pam would be joining me.

Then, with those two weeks nearly behind me, I began making arrangements for her arrival. We needed somewhere to stay temporarily until she got over the jet lag and then give us time to find somewhere to live. So, the first order of business was to book a room at the Cameron Hotel on Changi Road. This was where most newly arrived families stayed, so it was common knowledge that it catered almost exclusively to servicemen and their families. Next, was to apply for some leave to allow time for all of the above and to apply to Pay Accounts for "Living out allowance" to which married personnel living off camp were entitled.

The big day, 6th of January eventually arrived. I went to the Cameron Hotel and checked in and got the key to the room and then went up to check on it. The room was fairly basic but was clean. We didn't need much more than that. That night, I headed down to Paya Lebar airport in good time to be there when the British Eagle flight arrived. Going to the spectators' balcony, I saw it arrive and watched for Pam when she emerged. I waved but she didn't see me, so I hastily made my way to the Arrivals lounge. Eventually, passengers started trickling out of the Customs and Immigration area. I watched anxiously to catch a glimpse of her as anonymous people emerged, some greeted by waiting husbands while others were herded together by the Families staff. Finally, when it seemed that half of the plane's passenger load had been disgorged, she emerged from the Customs and Immigration exit looking beautiful despite the long time she had spent on board the Britannia. I waved to catch her attention and this time she saw me and sped up her pace as she hurried over to join me in a loving embrace. After some small talk about 'how was her flight' and 'how long had I been waiting' I picked up her suitcase and led her outside to be greeted by the warm, humid night air of Singapore. We took a taxi to the Cameron Hotel and soon settled in for the night because she was very tired after her trip. She told me that she had been "volunteered" to look after someone's child because the mother had other children to attend to.

The hotel room seemed a little different at night because it was lit by harsh fluorescent lights and the mattress on the bed was enveloped in a thick, clear plastic which didn't add to its comfort. But even so, those first few days was like a second honeymoon – and I'll leave it there.

Chapter 8: Cheviot Hill

We took it easy in the hotel for the next couple of days because of Pam's need to catch up on her jet lag. She had recovered sufficiently on her second day that we were able to do a little local sightseeing. Then, in the evening, we went to the restaurant in the Capitol building in the city to have a meal and see the Malayan cultural enactment that I had enjoyed a few months earlier. We had decided that on the third day we would look for somewhere to live. I had been given the name of a grocer on Frankel Avenue that rented fully furnished houses out to servicemen, so we set off to find him. He sent us with one of his employees to look at some houses and after seeing a few that we rejected, we settled on one on a street named Cheviot Hill. It contained all that we needed including bed linen and kitchenware. The grocer hinted strongly that we would purchase all our grocery needs from his shop. This was the same thing I had been told at the Families Office because, supposedly, the housing for living-out servicemen was scarce. But I had learned from others in the know that both were behind the times – the situation had subtly changed. After the cessation of hostilities with Indonesia, Britain, under Harold Wilson's Labour Government, had launched a withdrawal of HM Forces from the Far East and the reduction had already started happening in a big way. Now there were too many vacant houses chasing fewer potential tenants, so we didn't feel obliged to purchase overpriced goods from our grocer but shopped around for better prices elsewhere. That didn't stop the grocer from sending his boy to our door with pencil and paper, ready to take our order shortly after we moved in, but after being sent away a few times, the penny soon dropped, and he stopped coming.

The house on Cheviot Hill

Getting to work was now a different kettle of fish. Instead of the ten-minute stroll from the airmen's mess to the section that had been my custom up to now, I needed to leave home earlier and make my way several miles to get there. Not being in possession of a car, there needed to be another way to get there. Fortunately, in Singapore in those days, there was a tried-and-true solution – the pickup taxi. These taxis were unmistakeable from the other road users because of their distinctive colour scheme, a black body topped by a bright yellow roof.

Photo Credit: Facebook Group "Nostalgic Singapore"

The pickup taxis plied Changi Road and the East Coast Road, stopping along the way for anyone who signalled with a hand wave that they needed a ride. As a result, you would find yourself sharing the back seat with a variety of people, servicemen, their family members, or native Singaporeans. The fare was a modest few cents and, like a bus service, was determined by how far the passenger travelled, the increases being determined after the taxi passed certain points along the route. Also, there was no need to haggle over prices because there seemed to be an agreed fare structure observed by all drivers. Living at Cheviot Hill, I needed to walk just a few hundred yards west to Frankel Avenue, along which some taxis travelled to get from the Changi Road to the East Coast Road. This was a good place to get a taxi because it was far enough away from Changi that there were few, if any, passengers in the taxis heading in my direction, so it didn't take long for an empty one to come along. On the way, we picked up others until all seats were full, whereupon the driver often flogged his vehicle at kamikaze speed so that he could get there in time to be able to drop us off and look for other fares. For that reason, I always sat in the back seat and never up front with the driver. There were no seatbelts in those days, so that seat always seemed to be the suicide seat, in my humble opinion, although, in all fairness, I don't recall any of the taxis ever being involved in an accident.

One other thing I should mention – like most others, I always travelled armed with a black, rolled-up umbrella. This was because it wasn't unusual to be caught out in the open when a sudden tropical downpour of incredible intensity occurred. These rain showers were so heavy that they came straight down from the heavens, unaffected by any wind, and it was not uncommon to see a deluge falling on one side of a road while the opposite side was perfectly dry. Being caught in one of these localized showers without an umbrella would leave a person drenched to the skin, so although we may have looked like toffs with our rolled-up brollies, it was a sheer necessity, and just about everyone possessed one.

The umbrella I used while at Changi wasn't my first in the Far East but was an improvement on my Labuan model. Over there, life was a bit more rough and ready, so everyone used the local Asian bamboo and varnished paper variety. It was a cumbersome contraption, the handle and ribs made entirely of bamboo and the waterproof material that spanned between the ribs, which I think was paper, was heavily impregnated with what smelled strongly of the varnish or lacquer used to make it waterproof. They were bulky but served the purpose because the rain also plummeted down there, seemingly always at the same time in the early afternoon. I deliberately left my bamboo model behind when I left for Changi and purchased the more civilised rolled-up brolly shortly after arriving in Singapore.

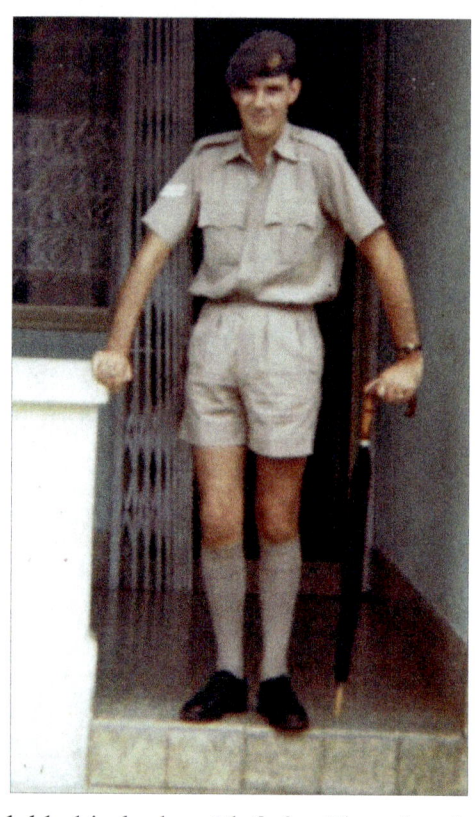

Returning home after work was a little different and easier. Instead of waiting at the roadside for a pickup taxi to come along, it was only necessary to take a short walk from the Electronics building out the Changi Road where the taxis were parked in a line on the verge at knockoff time, waiting for passengers. Mostly, they were the same drivers every day, so I came to recognize some of them and knew which were crazy kamikaze types who never used their brakes but always relied on honking the horn to get them out of trouble. In all fairness, that was typical of all traffic in Singapore. Maybe it's an exaggeration, but if I had bought a second-hand car on the island, it wouldn't have surprised me if the brakes were the original set and still in good condition, whereas the horn was dead or dying. My other preference was to choose a fairly recent Mercedes-Benz model instead of some the other makes or the older Mercedes models. That's because Mercedes-Benz advertised safety features that included a strengthened passenger compartment and a feature that, should the vehicle be involved in head-on crash, the engine was supposed to slide safely underneath the passenger compartment. The drivers of the newer Mercedes models were also usually more careful drivers. Fortunately, I was never in a situation where either of the Mercedes-Benz claims were put to the test.

If I were the first passenger getting into a taxi, I would tell the driver that I wanted the East Coast Road route, but if there were any others in the taxi, I would ask if it was going that way. Many of my workmates lived on the Opera Estate, which was nearer to the Changi Road, but past the turnoff for the East Coast Road, so it was important to make sure which route the taxi was taking. Nowadays, I believe that Singapore taxis are air-conditioned, but there was no such luxury in those days. Windows were all wound fully down, and I still have a mental image of hypnotically watching the hairs on my arm blowing backwards in the slipstream as it rested on the windowsill – full disclosure; I do have hairy arms.

Shortly after moving into the Cheviot Hill house, we were visited by a succession of local women, each looking for a job as our *amah*. That was the local word for a girl or woman employed by a family to clean, look after children, and perform other domestic tasks. The RAF included a sum of money in the living-out allowance for this purpose, and although we had no children, it was still a good idea to have someone to help around the house in such a hot climate. However, Pam didn't want a servant for all the housework, otherwise she would have nothing to do herself all day while I was at work, but she certainly felt that someone to help with the washing and ironing would be a blessing. One of the people who came to our door, (which is a figure of speech because they always came to the garden gate and waited to attract our attention), was a young, very pretty Chinese girl. I was all for hiring her, but that didn't go down well with the missus. Instead, she decided on an older, very plain woman. Obviously, I still had a lot to learn in my role as husband. Also, we only hired her for part-time work because there wasn't washing and ironing every day, although had she been full time, she could even have lived-in because there was an amah's quarter attached to the rear of the house, complete with Asian toilet.

For anyone not familiar with an Asian toilet, it is an item of plumbing, ceramic of course like a normal toilet, but set flush with the floor (no pun intended). There's a non-skid area on each side of this hole-in-the-ground where the user plants their feet as they squat over the opening to do their business.

Not long after moving in, we were surprised on several occasions at seeing a huge, dark-coloured rat in the backyard. The yard was all concrete and featured a trench about 6 inches deep and about the same across that extended from the back wall of the house all the way to the back gate. The function of this trench was to act as a drain – really a miniature monsoon drain that prevented the yard from flooding during heavy monsoonal downpours. Its unintended purpose, however, was to act as a runway for the rat, which used it as an escape route when it was disturbed. Pam refused to go out there by herself after it first surprised her, so I was always the one to see it. I tried to hit it by throwing things at it, but it was too fast and always ran along the trench and then vertically up the rear yard wall before disappearing. Pam insisted, as wives will, that I "do something" about it. So, after a few appearances by the obscene creature, I paid a visit to the section at Changi that specialized in keeping the station's pests in check (I don't recall its official name). They had an interesting display of many of the exotic bugs and rodents (dead and stuffed, of course) that had been caught over a long period of time. A knowledgeable sergeant gave me the gen on our particular pest. He explained that the rats had a favourite route that they stuck to. This could easily be seen by the greasy trail left by their fur. He then gave me a few small cellophane packets of what looked like Quaker Oats but explained that the oats were laced with warfarin. The oats, he said, were irresistible to rats but the warfarin made them thirsty to the extent that it caused them to go in search of water and keep drinking until they drowned. Just lay a few packets down on its greasy trail, he advised, and it will soon disappear. I was sceptical but followed his advice that night. The next morning, I went out into the yard first thing and saw that some of the oatmeal packets had disappeared, but better still, the rat disappeared too and although I fully expected it to show up again, it never did, much to Pam's relief.

    As a side note, while writing the above rat's tale, I thought it might be a good idea to make sure the warfarin remedy was correct, and so did a little research. It turns out that warfarin is indeed a deadly rat poison, but the drinking-until-they-drown part can be politely described as male bovine excrement. Warfarin is a powerful blood thinner and prevents the rat's blood from clotting to the extent that it suffers death from internal bleeding.

* * *

During my time in the Service, the Electrical Section on any station was responsible for providing electricians to the various squadrons on the station and to provide cover when a squadron electrician was on leave or absent for any other reason. And so, not long after we had taken up residence in Cheviot Hill, I was "volunteered" for this duty. I have two distinct memories of this temporary detachment.

The first one was at the large pan – a wide expanse of concrete – on the western side of the Changi Road. It was a very noticeable area because the Changi Road featured an aircraft crossing from the airfield on the eastern side of the road at that location. It was a common occurrence for traffic on the road to be brought to a halt when an aircraft needed to taxi or be towed from the airfield side to the pan, or vice versa. The traffic's progress was temporarily blocked by two red and white striped barriers that were lowered, one on each side of the taxiway, like the arms on a level crossing. The pan was home to 48 Squadron's Hastings and the Changi based Royal New Zealand Air Force 41 Squadron's Bristol Freighters as well as the area where visiting aircraft were received. On this occasion, I was detailed to fill in for a 48 Squadron corporal electrical fitter, who was off on leave, and was tasked with curing a snag on one of the Hastings. Two locally recruited Chinese airmen were detailed to assist me. I don't recall the nature of the snag, but being unfamiliar with the Hastings electrical system, I sought out the Hastings maintenance manual, better known as an Air Publication, or more commonly, the AP, (there's an AP for everything in the RAF). The two local airmen were interested in how I went about diagnosing the fault, so I showed them the circuit diagram in the AP and then the steps we needed to take to isolate its source, and then identify the location of the failed component on the aircraft. I got the firm impression that they had never been shown how to do anything like this and that the regular airmen they normally worked with treated them as general dogsbodies whom they assigned to do the grunt work, such as changing batteries or other heavy lifting. From the AP, I was able to determine that the faulty component was an electrical contactor located under the aisle in the passenger compartment. and was accessed through a hatch in the floor. I set the two airmen to remove it while I ordered a replacement from Stores and then had them install the new one. We performed a functional test after I had checked their work and then all three of us then went the squadron office to "clear" the fault in the Form 700. This was achieved by inserting an entry that briefly described the action we took to cure the snag, which I then over-signed as the supervising NCO. The two lads seemed grateful, but I had no idea just how grateful they were. To me, it was just a normal part of my responsibilities to mentor junior airmen, but the next day, one of them invited Pam and me to come to their home at the weekend to meet his parents. Visiting a Chinese home was a new experience for both of us, so we were a little reticent about it, but felt it would be ill mannered to turn down the invitation.

    We arrived at the young airman's address where he greeted us as we approached the open doorway. We noticed several pairs of flip-flops lined up neatly on the doorstep and knowing that it was an Asian custom to remove footwear before entering someone's home we started taking ours off. An older person inside called out, "No, no, don't need to take shoes off." We carried on taking them off anyway, because it would have made us feel uncomfortable to keep them on, knowing about their custom. The old gentleman offered no further objections, so we felt that we had done the right thing. Once over the threshold, we were guided to sit on two straight-backed chairs. The parents were seated across from us, and two or three other younger people were present. The conversation was a bit difficult because of the father's stilted English, but he asked us some polite questions about how we liked Singapore and where we came from in the UK. Sometimes our young host explained some of the things we said in Chinese to his parents because they clearly didn't understand us all the time and likewise, he interpreted some of the things his dad said, probably because he could read the puzzled look on our faces. Shortly after arriving, one of the younger people brought us some chilled water and some snacky stuff to nibble at. The visit didn't last too long, just enough to be polite without causing offence by leaving too soon. We thanked the parents for their hospitality and they, in turn, thanked us for coming, but Pam and I were both relieved when the visit was over because we had both felt very uncomfortable being in such a different cultural environment.

The next day, I thanked the young airman for inviting us and for the family's hospitality towards us and, to return the favour, invited him and his fellow local airman to our abode the following weekend. They both arrived at the appointed time, and it was a much more relaxed experience. They were both very curious about life in the UK and asked a lot of questions. At one point, the subject of decorating came up – in Singapore, all internal walls are painted – so they were highly amused when we said that wallpapering was the typical method of decorating room walls back in England. They seemed to think it was strange that British people stuck paper on the internal walls of their houses and laughed incredulously at the thought. I don't know what they imagined, but we couldn't believe they had been unaware of that fact, although, in reflection, I never saw wallpaper anywhere in Singapore in those days.

The second memory was of a time soon after. I don't know now why I kept getting these temporary detachments, but maybe it was because I was new to the Section and got volunteered because of being low man on the totem pole. Or perhaps there was a roster that had each of us on standby for a certain length of time. Whatever the reason, it's lost to me now, but this detachment was for one week to what I believe must have been Station Flight, which handled all visiting aircraft. It should have been on the concrete pan where I had had the earlier experience, but not so. The big difference was that Changi's runway was out of service for maintenance at the time, so Station Flight was temporarily detached to RAF Tengah on the far side of the Singapore island. It was about 15 miles from Cheviot Hill, around three times as far as Changi. The only way to get there was by taxi – not pickup taxi because there was no regular route from where I lived to Tengah, so it meant hailing a taxi and negotiating a price. Most of the drivers would quote a fare that was very much higher than what it should have been, but not surprising for Singapore in that era. The way around being swindled was to insist on them doing the trip "on the meter," which all Singapore taxis had to have by law. On this detachment, I was on the night shift, so I had to leave Pam at home by herself after dark.

The incident that comes to mind is from a night when we were seeing off an RAF VC10 that was flying repatriated servicemen and their families back to RAF Lyneham. This was a short time after Pam and I had both travelled out to Singapore by British Eagle Airways, so the VC10 service must have started shortly afterwards. Anyway, to resume the story – the incoming flight had been late in arriving, so the frustrated outgoing passengers had been hanging around for a long time, some of them with small, whining children. Finally, with the families all aboard, the doors were closed, the mobile stairway had been wheeled away and all four engines were up and running. The VC10 seemed ready to taxi out, but then all four engines were shut down. Not a good sign! The Flight office was then informed by the tower that there was a problem with jet pipe temperature indication for one of the starboard engines. This, I knew from my Vulcan experience, was a problem with the jet-pipe temperature (JPT) control system for the engine – an electrical problem that my trade would have to sort out.

The order came for the passengers to temporarily disembark so that we could get on board to sort things out. The stairway was wheeled back in place and the door opened by the cabin staff. Anxious to get working on the snag, a sergeant, an airman and I raced up the stairway. The sergeant was familiar with the VC10 electrical system, whereas I was not, so he knew where the JPT control system components were located at the rear of the aircraft to be near the engines. In our haste to get on with the job, we made our way down the aisle towards the rear of the passenger cabin, squeezing past the fed-up looking disembarking passengers like salmon swimming upstream, some of them were carrying sleeping children in their arms. Much to my surprise, the sergeant led us into the cramped interior of the rear, starboard toilet. I couldn't see how the controller could be anywhere in there, but I wasn't prepared for what he did next. The sergeant pushed on one end of a black sign that read "NO SMOKING" in white lettering, mounted at eye level on the wall opposite the sink.

Amazingly, the end of the label that he pushed on rotated into the wall around a midway pivot point, revealing that it was really a cunningly disguised panel fastener. When he had pushed it in as far as it would go and it was at right angles to the wall, he then pulled on the other end, which was jutting out of the recess. Lo and behold, the wall divided into two sections that he then folded back, concertina style, revealing a large compartment containing various electrical and electronic "black boxes," cable looms together with various pipes and tubing. (Maybe I shouldn't be giving away these trade secrets). Two JPT Amplifiers, one per engine for the starboard side, were mounted in this compartment. Although "black boxes" is the generally accepted terms for enclosed box-like electrical/electronic equipment these were, in fact, shiny, stainless-steel boxes, each about the size of a shoe box.

Sarge left us in order to get a serviceable replacement from stores and bring it back together with a test set that we would need to calibrate the replacement unit, once it was installed. Meanwhile, the airman and I set about disconnecting and removing the "snagged" amplifier. It wasn't an easy job because the box wasn't bolted directly to the airframe. Instead, its four hold-down bolts were fastened to four anti-vibration mountings for the protection of the delicate electronics inside. Trying to undo the bolts holding the box to these mountings was like trying to spoon-feed medicine to a squirming toddler. Both tasks required the cooperation of two people. In the case of the amplifier, one of us had to hold the box steady while the other unscrewed the bolts. Meanwhile, the Air Quartermaster (AQM) kept popping his head into the cramped "khazi" to check on our progress, before disappearing again, presumably to keep the captain informed.

When the sergeant returned, we installed the new item and, after making all the necessary connections, plugged in the calibration set to a special socket on the end of the box. Having done that, we informed the AQM and asked him to pass on a request to the captain to run the engine so that we could perform the calibration. Shortly afterwards, we heard the loud cracking noises of the engine igniters firing off their high voltage sparks that would ignite the fuel in the engine combustion chamber, followed by the initial low-pitched whine that increased steadily in frequency and decibel level until the engine settled down at idling speed. The calibration process wasn't something that could be hurried, the sergeant explained. First, it was necessary to wait for the engine to "heat soak" – this could be compared to warming a car engine up on a cold day. While this was going on, the AQM hung around at the toilet doorway, wearing a headset by which he was keeping the flight deck crew informed of our progress.

At some point, the sergeant decided that the engine was warm enough for him to proceed with the calibration. There then followed a series of requests from the sergeant to the flight deck, relayed by the AQM, for various levels of engine speed. As this was happening, the sergeant adjusted a couple of potentiometers on the amplifier while carefully watching the meter on the test set. Eventually he and the captain were satisfied with the settings, so he disconnected the test set. We then tidied up, making sure there were no tools or loose objects left behind, before folding the wall back into place and locking it by pushing down on the "NO SMOKING" sign until it snapped into place, flush with the wall. Back in the office, we "cleared" the snag on the "travelling" Form 700, which was then picked up by the AQM to take back to the aircraft.

Before leaving, the AQM confided that an army Major, who was a passenger on the VC10 and was the designated officer in charge of the returning flight, had complained to the captain that we had pushed our way onto the aircraft too soon, instead of waiting for the passengers to disembark, expressing his dissatisfaction that our sweaty bodies had been brushing past everyone on our way to rear of the aircraft. We hadn't been aware of the presence of the Major because all military passengers aboard the aircraft had been dressed in civilian clothes, as required by the RAF because the VC10 would be making stops in foreign countries on its return journey. Nor did the Major speak to us directly. However, the AQM let us know that he and the flight deck crew quietly approved of our prompt attention to fixing the problem, especially since they were already a few hours behind schedule.

Chapter 9: Rose Garden

After having seen the VC10 off, we were stood down for the evening. I made my way to Tengah's front gate where a few taxis were queued up waiting for customers and got into the one that was next in line. After the usual dickering over the fare, he agreed to charge by the taximeter and drove me back to Cheviot Hill. I don't remember exactly if it was the same night, or some other night, but I was surprised to see Pam outside on the front porch when I arrived. It was dark, after all, so this seemed very unusual. Seeing the puzzled look on my face, she explained that she had been sitting reading on the rattan sofa in the living room, when a scratching noise coming from the ceiling alarmed her. Looking up, she caught a glimpse of something trying to pull up a corner of one of the green-painted plywood ceiling panels. Just as soon as she looked up, the panel dropped back into place and noise stopped, but the unusual activity scared her. She thought maybe a cat had got trapped up there, and then the memory of the big black rat that she had seen in the backyard, which had run up a wall and disappeared, came to mind. In any case, whatever it was gave her the willies, so she decided to wait for me outside.

I went into the house to have a look around while she remained on the porch, but nothing seemed out of place and there was no indication of anything unusual. I checked all the rooms and went out into the backyard, but nothing there seemed to be out of the ordinary, so I went back out onto the front porch and encouraged her to come back into the house with me. She was a little reluctant, but we both went back inside. Nothing else happened that night, nor in the next few days and there was no indication of rat activity, so Pam gradually relaxed.

Our next-door neighbours were a nice Chinese couple and, a few days after her night-time scare, Pam was talking to the woman, who had some bad news to share. Some nights previously, while she and her husband were out celebrating Chinese New Year, their home was burgled and much of her jewellery had been stolen. Apparently, the burglar had removed some of the roof tiles and had got into the house that way. She asked if we had been burgled, but Pam told her that we hadn't. But it worried Pam that this had happened, as she made clear to me that evening while telling me about the neighbour's misfortune. Thankfully, my temporary detachment had come to an end, and I was back in the Electrical Section again, working normal 8 to 5 days. In retrospect, the neighbours' experience should have rung an alarm bell with us in view of what happened later but, for some reason, it didn't at the time.

It was monsoon season, and several days after the now-forgotten ceiling incident, the heavens opened and stayed open for at least a whole day during which torrential rain poured down on Singapore. The pick-up taxi ride home was a sloshing affair with lots of spray thrown up by the other vehicles on the roads, making visibility very poor, although it didn't discourage the driver from putting a heavy foot on the accelerator for a nail-biter of a trip along Changi Road. When I got to Cheviot Hill, trusty umbrella protecting me from the never-ending deluge, I found Pam in an agitated state and for good reason. Water was running down the wall that divided the living room from the kitchen. It wasn't a trickle – it was sheet of water. Obviously, we had a seriously leaking roof. Somehow I managed to get up to roof level, probably by standing on a chair. Sheltering under my trusty umbrella, I was able to get high enough to see if there was any obvious reason for the problem. What an understatement that is! There, on the shallowly sloping roof, was a neatly stacked pile of roof tiles alongside a gaping hole big enough for a man to climb through. And apparently, that's exactly what had happened. It's conjecture, of course, but it would seem that the neighbour's burglar had also paid us an uninvited visit by the same means that he had gained access to their house. Apparently, he was the type that didn't tidy up after himself, and now a river of monsoonal rainwater was pouring down through the gaping hole he had made in the roof.

Getting up on the roof was impossible, and it would have been slippery and treacherous anyway, so there was nothing I could do about closing up the hole there and then. Climbing down from my makeshift perch, I went inside to let Pam know what was causing the leak. Her reaction was explosive, to say the least, because she now realized that it hadn't been rat or cat that had pulled the ceiling panel up as she sat vulnerably by herself. To put it mildly, she did not feel in any way secure in that house and demanded that I "do something about it!"

The next morning, I went to work as usual, but promised Pam that I would go to the Families Office to see if they could help in any way. Shortly after arriving, I told Sergeant Jackson-Smith about our experience. He was completely sympathetic and encouraged me to go and talk to the Families people. So, I walked across to the Families Office and soon got the ear of the sergeant, telling him about the attempted burglary and the problem with the rain pouring into the house as a result. Also, that my wife was feeling very insecure and wanted to move. I didn't know what he would recommend but was completely and pleasantly surprised when he offered to move us to an RAF Hiring.

A Hiring is the equivalent of a Married Quarter, except that it is privately owned, and the owner has entered into a contract with the RAF to allow the property to be rented to RAF married personnel. The occupant pays a standard married quarters rent to the RAF who, in turn, pays the owner a negotiated rent. To be accepted as a Hiring, the property, whether it be a house or a flat, must meet certain standards and must be furnished with the basic necessities of a home, including bed linen, cutlery, cooking utensils and crockery to the extent that a family, or a couple such as us, could move in and have every basic essential for a comfortable home.

In our case, the Hiring was a two-bedroom flat in a fairly modern complex known as Rose Garden, in the Katong district. The flat was vacant, so we were able to move in the very next day – Sergeant Jackson-Smith had generously allowed me the time off to make the move, although we didn't have much to move – just a suitcase each. The flat was on the top floor of a four-storey apartment building. Access was by stairs only, but we were a young couple, so climbing four flights of stairs wasn't too much of a problem.

The flat (arrowed) in Rose Garden

The flat had a nice clean appearance – light coloured mosaic tiled floors throughout, which would be easy to keep clean. A balcony adjacent to the living room was accessed through a glass paned door that, along with large, louvred windows, allowed light to pour into the interior. This balcony overlooked a grassy common area between ours and another identical building in the complex. A second balcony on the opposite side of the building opened off the kitchen. The waist-high metal railing of the balcony had four metal tubes, about one foot long and around two inches in diameter, sticking at an upward angle of some thirty degrees outwards from just below the top rail. A stout bamboo pole was inserted into each of these holders – the Singapore equivalent of a clothesline for multi-storey flats. We knew this because many of our neighbours were obviously using them for that purpose. This balcony overlooked the Singapore Strait – a busy shipping lane. On the other side of the Strait, we could see Batam

Island, which is Indonesian territory. Both front and back balconies were surrounded by a steel grill to deter burglars, but each had a lockable section that could be opened, in the form of two gates, for safety reasons but also, in the case of the rear balcony, to allow access to the bamboo pole holders.

Amber Road, the street that bordered the west side of the complex, led to the beach, only a short distance away at that time, and there was a large kampong on the other side of the street.

We "marched in" to the Hiring just as we would have done had it been a proper RAF married-quarter house. A corporal from the Families Office met us at the front door at a pre-arranged time and then we walked through each room of the flat making notes of any damage. There was no "marching" involved – the expression was a hang-over from earlier times when a serviceman and his family were literally marched into a married quarter and then marched out when they vacated it, this was just a casual walk through the flat. However, it was important to make sure all damage, no matter how small, was noted because a similar walk-through would take place when we "marched-out" and if any damages were found that hadn't been noted during the march-in, we would be charged the cost to put them right. This actually happened to us when we marched-out at the end of my tour, but I'm getting ahead of myself and will talk about that at the appropriate point.

Once we accepted the Hiring and I had signed for it, we were free to move in. With the keys in our possession, Pam and I made our way back to the Cheviot Hill residence and started the process of moving out. We needed to spend one more night there, to pack our meagre belongings, clean the place up and pay off the Amah when she came next morning. Having done all that and making sure that we had everything before locking the door behind us, we set off for Rose Garden, stopping on the way at our grocer landlord's shop to drop off the Cheviot Hill house keys and inform him about the displaced roof tiles. He wasn't exactly thrilled to receive either of those items of news, but there was little he could do but scowl. That done, we headed to our new abode and unpacked.

It wasn't too long before there was a knock on the door. When I opened it, a Malay woman stood there and asked if we needed an Amah. News had apparently travelled swiftly over to the kampong across the road because that was where she was from. She seemed a steady sort of woman and agreed to just doing the laundry and ironing – Pam was going to take care of keeping the flat clean herself, just as she'd done at Cheviot Hill, so we hired her.

Life was a little different at Rose Garden than it had been at Cheviot Hill. We were surrounded by more people than before. Most of the other flat residents were Chinese, although there were some who looked more or less like we did, if you know what I mean, but not necessarily British. For example, the flat directly across from us was occupied by a middle-aged Russian man who had a young Chinese girl living with him, and I don't think she was the Amah. In the picture above, you might have noticed two very young, white children. We didn't know them – they just happened to be in the camera shot. Our next-door neighbours were also Chinese, and although polite, they barely passed the time of day with us when we happened to meet on the stairs.

Numerous food vendors arrived daily and patrolled the complex on bicycle-powered trishaws that had a box-like container mounted on the front axle instead of a seat. The Malay word for food is *makan* (pronounced mah-can), so we called them the *makan*-men. Each vendor seemed to specialize in some kind of prepared dish and announced their presence by clacking two bamboo sticks together, each of them having a specific rhythmic phrasing, so that the residents would know when a favourite dish had arrived. For those in the flats above the ground floor, the method of purchasing anything was to shout down their order and then lower a bucket on a rope with the money inside and an empty dish. The vendor then ladled out the food into the dish, giving the customer the signal to haul up when the transaction was complete. Other vendors plied the complex, including one that sold baked goods. We patronized this one to buy bread, using the same rope and bucket method as our neighbours, (a bucket with a length of rope tied to its handle had been thoughtfully included in the flat's furnishings). He amused us because every day he would sing-song up to us, "You want any sausage roll, curry puff?" We always declined, but that never stopped him from asking.

***

Washing draped from the bamboo poles of multiple flats was a daily spectacle in Rose Garden, it looked like bunting that one might see during the celebration of special occasions in the U.K., although most of it was not as colourful as bunting. We were no exception to this practice because clothing needs to be washed more frequently in hot, humid climates. We didn't have a washing machine, so the Amah did it by hand in the kitchen sink, although Pam washed her "unmentionables" herself when the Amah wasn't there.

A few months after we moved into the flat, I found another use for the bamboo pole holders. It was a case of necessity. As mentioned earlier, we dangled the bucket-on-a-rope down from the back balcony to purchase bread from the bakery vendor, but one day the neighbour living on the ground floor flat directly below ours had a fixed aluminium awning installed. Besides providing him with a sunshade, the neighbour was probably fed up with having water that drained from the balconies above raining down and finding its way into his flat. This was understandable, because upper floor occupants sluiced down their tiled balconies with water, which then poured earthwards from a drain hole at the edge of the balconies. Some of it splashed onto the ground floor occupant's patio, so the awning acted to divert the water outwards and away from the building. But the awning was directly in the path of the buckets of those of us in the flats directly above. When the baker man next arrived, the flat's occupant, a rotund Chinese man, came out and adopted a combative stance while glaring up at me as if to say, "Go on, just try it!"

Blast it! I had to trot down four flights of stairs to make the purchase and then climb back up again with the bread. "Bugger that for a joke!" I thought. So, what could I do to avoid having to make the same trip in future? Pondering over the problem for some time, trying to use the initiative the RAF had always encouraged its members to employ, (imagine you're hearing the RAF March playing in the background just about now). My eyes landed on the broom Pam used to sweep the floor. Wondering if it would work, I stuck the shaft into one of the bamboo holders. It fitted snugly into the holder and appeared to go out far enough to clear the neighbour's awning. Next, I removed the broom from the pole holder and passed the rope over the centre of the broom-head. Now with the bucket dangling below the broom-head, I relocated the shaft into the holder. So far, so good! Slowly paying out the rope, I watched to see if it would in fact clear the awning and miracle of miracles, it did!

A few days later, when the baker-man returned and announced his presence below, I put the broom and bucket arrangement into operation. By this time, the ground floor neighbour was already outside, looking every bit as combative as he had on the previous occasion, keeping his beady eye on me. After calling down my order for a loaf, (no sausage roll or curry puff, thank you), I began lowering the bucket with the cash inside. The neighbour became increasingly apoplectic as the bucket slowly came down, but then turned it down a couple of notches when he saw that the bucket had cleared his precious awning. He wasn't altogether pleased, but at least he didn't appear to be about to blast off into orbit. The baker-man on the other hand, laughed loudly and gave me the thumbs-up sign. The transaction proceeded successfully, and we continued to use the broom and bucket method from then onwards.

Chapter 10: Rusty

Back at work, several of us who lived off-camp spent our lunchtime break in the snack bar run by the sullen Chinese lad and his even more sullen sister, although the food they served up wasn't bad. In fact, it was as much a crew room as a snack bar. The chairs that we used were "rattan" – shaped bamboo frames with strips of bamboo used in a wickerwork-like manner to form the seats and back rests. The result was a strong, lightweight chair. Besides accommodating our rear ends, the seats also harboured a thriving community of small roaches. Maybe it's where the larger roaches – the ones we regularly saw scurrying around in monsoon drains and occasionally in our homes and other places – laid their eggs. Anyway, sometimes, just for the hell of it, one of us would pick up a chair, which was fairly light, and bang it back down hard on the floor. Without fail, a multitude of little roaches of various sizes would drop out from the seat bottom and scurry around the snack bar floor, much to the consternation of the fuming couple behind the counter.

During lunchbreaks and often at other times in the day, a few men would sit around chatting, taking the mickey telling jokes – normal crew room behaviour. Sometimes we would talk shop until someone commented, "Shut the hangar doors!" But talking shop included mentioning our prior history in the service and I no doubt spoke of my time on Vulcans.

We had the usual cross-section of personalities that you would find in any community, including the "village idiot." In our group, the "VI" was a ground electrician nicknamed Rusty. Maybe it's unfair to label him an idiot, but he was certainly immature and impressionable, a lightweight to whom no one paid much attention, except to scoff at some of his utterances. But then he started coming to work wearing obviously new, expensive-looking wristwatches that he flashed around and made sure everyone saw them. It wasn't just one or two watches, but more like a new one each day for several days running. Naturally, many of us wondered what was behind all of this parade of watches. Rusty wasn't secretive about it, rather he was eager to tell us about the Saudi Arabian prince who had befriended him and, being very rich, splashed out to buy his new pal these fancy timepieces. The prince, we were told was in Singapore because he was a Saudi Arabian diplomat. It didn't stop there, though. Rusty claimed that his prince, who he referred to as Hamid, was eager to make friends with those of us in Rusty's circle of acquaintances – "Wouldn't you like to meet a Saudi prince, Brian?" he asked me one day. It seemed that this Hamid person held court for his pals at the Ocean Park Hotel on the East Coast Road. This was a popular watering hole that regularly put on very enjoyable outdoor entertainment. It also had a ten-pin bowling alley that was popular with many service people and Hamid was happy to hang around there, footing the bill for drinks and other treats.

I let Rusty know that I had no desire to join the group, and in my view, Saudi princes were ten-a-penny. Inwardly, my alarm bells were ringing as I know they were for a few others in our group. Having spent most of my service, up until then, in the hyper security conscious V-force, where the tactics of foreign intelligence gatherers were frequently drummed into us until it became embedded within our sub-conscious, I could sense that Rusty was being groomed for nefarious purposes. I also knew that Saudi Arabia wasn't a potential enemy of Britain, which meant that Hamid was working for someone else. Speaking amongst ourselves, several of us concluded that he was working for the Russians or the Chinese. As mentioned earlier, Changi at that time was the home of 215 Squadron's Shackletons that hunted for Russian and Chinese submarines over a wide area around Singapore. A lot of electronic equipment that the Shacks operated in the course of their mission was secret – I had actually serviced one piece of this equipment in the electrical bay that was used to literally sniff the exhaust fumes given off by diesel powered subs.

Whoever Hamid was working for, it became very obvious to me one day that he had set Rusty on an intelligence gathering mission. I was alone in the snack bar when Rusty entered and, on seeing me there, came over and sat down at my table. Not being very subtle, he asked me to tell him about the ECM (Electronic Counter Measures) installed on the Vulcan, knowing full well from general crewroom chatter that I had been involved with this aircraft. His request was in reference to the then state-of-the-art radar jamming equipment that was designed to confuse enemy radar during the Cold War. The equipment had the appearance of several dustbin-like "cans" housed within the bulbous protrusion at the tail end of the Vulcan. Truth to tell, I knew next to nothing about ECM other than a few of the code names by which it was known, and the location of the "cans" mentioned above. But for the benefit of Rusty, I pretended not to understand by asking him if he was talking about the "European Common Market." It took a bit of deadpanning for a while, on my part, before he got the message that there was nothing to be gained in flogging this dead horse, so he gave up and wandered off.

Many years later, I learned that indeed there was a Saudi prince-cum-diplomat in Singapore named Hamid. The information I received included his full name, but I would rather not include it here because someone of the same name currently lives in Singapore. However, it is true that he really was a Saudi diplomat. My informant told me that Hamid had the reputation of being able to "charm ducks off water." It turned out that he was under surveillance by the SIB (the military Special Investigations Branch), which was very much aware of his activities in attempting to gain information about RAF activities in that part of the world. Hamid was supposedly gathering intelligence for his Muslim Indonesian brethren, with whom Britain had been in conflict up until shortly prior to my arrival into FEAF. Of course, the hostilities had ceased by the time Hamid was playing footsy with Rusty, so one wonders if he had found another client – the Chinese perhaps.

Given that information, it's a sure bet that Rusty's association with Hamid was no secret to the SIB. But who knows what really goes on in the dark corners of intelligence and counterintelligence? Of course, it's possible that Rusty might have been a plant by the SIB and his job was not only to play along with Hamid but, at the same time, find out who in his circle of acquaintances were likely to divulge classified information. I'll never know, but I have a vague recollection that Rusty "disappeared" and by that, I don't mean something bad happened to him – just that he was posted somewhere else.

Chapter 11: Katong

Katong could best be described as a village on the outskirts of Singapore city. It straddled a wide road that underwent a sudden name change from 'Mountbatten Road' to 'East Coast Road,' (when traveling eastwards), where it intersected with Amber Road. The Rose Garden complex occupied the large plot of land on the corner of East Coast Road and Amber Road and the Katong commercial district began just beyond the Rose Garden blocks of flats. It bordered each side of the road, beginning with two cinemas that were almost opposite each other. On our side of the street, the cinema screened films that emanated from British and American studios, whereas the one on the opposite side showed martial arts films that were churned out by the Shaw Brothers, some of which were shot locally, whilst others were filmed in Hong Kong. Naturally, we patronized the one that showed films in which the cast spoke English, regardless of whether it was with an English or American accent. It was there that we saw the James Bond "*Thunderball*" film that had its early scenes shot on location at Waddington, my old station, and featured the Vulcan with which I had a strong association. Down a side street, just after the cinema, was the Coq d'Or, a French themed restaurant that we patronized, but more about it later.

Further along, there was a bank guarded on the outside by a Sikh night watchman. Sometimes, he was on his feet, but at other times, when things were quiet, he reclined on a contraption that looked like a bedstead. It didn't have a mattress and was essentially just a frame on four legs with a matrix of criss-crossed bamboo strips stretched between its four sides that would have supported a mattress. This was a common sight in Singapore – turbaned Indian Sikh nightwatchmen who seemed to have cornered that particular job market, because I never came across any others of different religion and ethnicity.

Continuing along in the same direction, the street on the north side was lined with several Chinese open-fronted kitchens that cooked small batches of food in woks over charcoal fires outside the kitchens. Customers sat around on stools, one hand holding a small china bowl close to the face while using chop sticks to stuff food into their mouths with the other. Leftovers were discarded into a large, deep, open monsoon drain that ran along the side of the narrow pavement where, down below, large rats and huge cockroaches gorged on the bounty that descended from above. At night, the cooks performed their culinary act by the light of Tilly lamps, bestowing a soft glow on the area.

Katong street scene, June 1967

Across the street we discovered a fish market where we often braved the pungent smells to purchase some fresh fish. It wasn't quite like going into the fishmonger back home and asking for a pound of cod fillet that would be weighed out on the shopkeeper's scale. Nothing like that! There was no cod, but we could buy a white fish with similar texture, although I forget the name – if I ever knew it in the first place. Nor could we ask for a pound of this fish. The unit of measurement was the *kati*, roughly equal to 1.33 pounds or 0.604 kg., and instead of a scale, the merchant produced what looked like a large chopstick that he dangled horizontally by one hand. A small, round, metal pan was suspended from one end of this rod, but there wasn't a similar pan on the other side. Instead, there was a small weight hanging by a short length of chain about a third of the way in from the end. The weight was free to slide along the rod. We learned later that this was a typical example of a traditional Chinese scale and was not too unusual throughout Singapore. This was just the first time we had seen one.

To weigh the fish, the merchant placed it in the pan and then slid the weight along the rod until it became horizontal. Graduations along the length of that end of the rod indicated to the merchant how much the item weighed, although there was no way that I could tell what weight the graduations represented. Walking further along brought us to several different shops and businesses. Amongst them, a bakery, and a few dress-making businesses that Pam patronised from time to time.

Traditional Chinese scale

A short time after we moved to Katong, a Western style supermarket opened to a great fanfare. Chinese make a big thing of launching a new business and this was no exception. There had been a lot of advance publicity about the opening ceremony, so we knew about it and went along to watch. At the appointed hour, a string of loud, Chinese firecrackers, suspended from an angled pole, announced the official opening. Then, two lion dancers took centre stage as they pranced around in time to the beats of a large drum mounted on what looked like a chariot. The supermarket entrance was filled with ornate arrangements of orchids, mounted on trestles, that had been placed there by other businesses by way of congratulations. The name of the supermarket was Tay Buan Guan, although the signage abbreviated it to TBG to make it easier for we foreigners.

Shopping in a familiar supermarket environment was much easier for us, where recognizable food items were arranged on shelves that were laid out in aisles. But like all the grocery shops in Singapore, there was no fresh meat. Only frozen meat, imported from Australia, was available. Still, it was better than the poky grocery shops that we had had to put up with until the coming of TBG. However, we did have a problem with that particular establishment a few months later, but this needs to be related against the background of some economic history, both British and Singaporean.

At the beginning of my tour in Singapore, the Malaysian dollar was the currency in use, even though Singapore had recently become independent of Malaysia. Shortly after Pam arrived, Singapore issued its own currency, the Singapore dollar, which was on a par with the Malayan & British Borneo dollar. Later that year, November 1967 to be precise, the Harold Wilson government suddenly devalued the Pound Sterling by 14%. We knew nothing of this when it first happened, but evidently, word had been passed to the Singapore business community. That day, Pam and I went shopping at TBG and paid in Singapore dollars with a large denomination note

We were given change in brand new Malayan & British Borneo dollars that looked as though they had just come off the printing press. It seemed a bit strange to me at the time, but I didn't think much to it because they were of the same value, or so I thought. A few days later, we went shopping again and since I had a wallet full of the Malayan currency, I offered them for payment. The merchant demanded more than the agreed dollar rate because, as he explained, the Malayan dollar was tied to the British Pound Sterling and was therefore something like 15% less in value whereas the Singapore dollar stayed at its original value. Years later, while researching for this story, I discovered that the new Singapore dollar was also linked to the Pound Sterling when first issued, so I don't quite understand the difference in the values and can only conclude that we had been "done" although it wasn't just one merchant – it was universal. I tried to have them accepted at face value at other establishments but without success, so had to eventually accept the devaluation.

Katong today from the same viewpoint
(Google earth "street scene")

I can't leave the topic of Katong without mentioning Le Coq D'Or restaurant that we found in a little back street near Rose Garden. It may have been a hotel, but I only recall the restaurant. Nor do I recall how we discovered it but seem to think it was from local advertising. Regardless, it became our favourite place for celebrating special occasions. And what was so special about it? I'm glad you asked. Well, it had a very intimate atmosphere – subdued lighting, not too many other diners, and enhanced by a talented songstress who, backed by a small formally-dressed trio of musicians, entertained us with standard favourites at a volume that was enjoyable whilst not being intrusive to conversation. But that wasn't the main attraction – in those days, the only red meat available to us was frozen solid and lacked much in the way of flavour, but at Le Coq D'Or they served tender, delicious, fresh fillet steaks that had never been frozen, which were flown in daily from Australia. Then, there was the special way they had of serving them. After placing our order for the steaks, we enjoyed an adult beverage while being entertained by the singer and her trio for maybe half an hour. All of a sudden, the kitchen door would slam open with a bang and a small procession of servers would approach our table, pushing a cart bearing our meals. The steaks, sizzling on dangerously hot, cast-iron platters that were recessed into scorched wooden holders, were then ceremoniously placed before us and, as a final touch, a knob of butter placed on top of each with a dramatic flourish, the butter quickly melting. The servers then quickly retreated. The steaks, understandably piping hot, almost melted in the mouth, they were so juicily delicious. It was a meal to die for!

Chapter 12: Work & Play

Getting to work at the E&I Section at RAF Changi was a lot easier from Rose Garden than it had been from Cheviot Hill. It took just a short walk out onto the East Coast Road. Traffic in Singapore drives on the left-hand side, just like at home, so that meant I had to cross to the other side of the street to catch a pickup taxi. Luckily, Rose Garden seemed to be the starting point for pickup taxi passengers, so I was usually the first to get aboard and be able to choose where to sit. Usually, this was directly behind the driver because it meant not having to shuffle along later when the driver picked up other passengers. Of course, as mentioned earlier, I avoided sitting in the front, beside the driver. Although none of the taxis I ever rode in was involved in an accident, it would have meant being a fair degree clairvoyant to know that it wasn't going to happen on any given trip, there or back. Others must have felt the same way because it was always the last passenger to be picked up who earned the dubious honour of riding shotgun.

Driving through Katong and along the East Coast Road, the driver stopped whenever he spied an obvious passenger – one that was usually hailing him with his rolled-up brolly. And so, we sped along until Bedok Junction where the road took a sharp left-hand turn and ceased to be the East Coast Road. We were now on a short stretch known as Bedok Road – the "k" wasn't pronounced for some reason, so it sounds like "Bee-doh." Bedok Road intersected with Changi Road that carried much more traffic, most of which was heading east in the direction of Changi. Soon we passed the Cameron Hotel, where Pam and I had stayed following her arrival in Singapore, and then, getting close to RAF Changi, we passed the sinister, grim grey edifice of Changi Prison that had been used by the Japanese to hold Allied prisoners of war during their occupation of the island. It was still in use, but now for civilian prisoners who had been jailed for serious offences.

Changi prison

There was a kampong almost opposite the prison and I remember we often picked up one of my workmates at that location. He was an ex-Apprentice, on his first posting after passing out from Halton. He had met a local girl and was shacked up with her in the kampong. It was oddly amusing to see him standing there at the edge of the kampong in his KD uniform, rolled up brolly in hand when kampong dwellers milled all around him. What made him stand out even more is that he was blessed, or maybe cursed, with a head of bright red hair, so he could definitely not have been taken for a local amongst all those dark-haired individuals. Naturally, he got the shotgun seat.

Closer to Changi, we came upon the aircraft "level crossing," which was usually open but, on occasions, the red and white striped barriers were down to halt the road traffic while an aircraft taxied across the road from the runway side of the airfield to the pan on the western side. Then it was up a small rise, past the Chartered Bank, (where Pay Accounts deposited my hard-earned Singapore dollars into my account), which brought us to the junction of Changi Road and Tangmere Road, the latter being the main entrance into the RAF Changi domestic site.

In the centre of the junction stood a locally recruited RAF policeman atop a wooden box-like plinth. He was attired in the usual KD uniform, which was otherwise unremarkable, except that he was wearing a white pith helmet instead of the usual white SD hat that normal RAF police wore. His job was to direct traffic at the junction, which again was unremarkable, except that he performed this duty with highly exaggerated military precision. His arm movements, waving traffic to move along the Changi Road were stiff and precise. Then, when he indicated that this traffic was to halt, he performed a left turn on top of the plinth that would have brought tears of joy to a drill instructor's eyes and warmth to his heart. In completing the turn, he stamped his left foot down on the top of the plinth with a resounding crash that made me wonder if it would smash a hole in the structure. This performance was repeated when he turned back to direct the Changi Road flow to resume. Soon after passing through the junction, we passed the post office and then arrived at the outskirts of Changi Village, where the E&I Section was located a short distance on the airfield side of Farnborough Road. It was here that I, and the others paid the driver and then got out of the taxi.

A short walk east on Felixstowe Road, in the direction of the hangars and the airfield, took me to the Electronics Squadron building. I would like to be able to tell you about all the exciting things that went on inside there, but the truth is that working there was a very mundane, 8 to 5 job. What we did in the E&I Section was take in electrical and instrument components that had been removed from the squadron aircraft because they were either unserviceable or were due for routine servicing. As I've already mentioned earlier, we had two or three local men to do the dirty work of stripping down aircraft generators and alternators. We, the RAF staff, were mostly responsible for the clean work, things like fault finding, calibration and the testing of the serviced components. It could be that the most exciting thing that happened to me was the day a coupling that connected a generator to the generator test rig broke while I was spinning the genny at its rated speed. Mick, an SAC who helped with the testing, marvelled later at how quickly I disappeared down behind a work bench as coupling parts flew around the room.

Or, maybe it was the day that Singapore's Prime Minister, Lee Kuan Yew, strolled through the section along with an escort of Brass and nodded to me as I stood at attention. That's not a joke – we, the British, were on the point of pulling out of Singapore in keeping with the Harold Wilson government's policy of reducing our overseas presence. The Singapore government was shaking in its collective boots, wondering how they were going to survive after the cash cow had left the farm. The British presence – the Naval dockyard at the north part of the island and all the other military bases provided a significant, if not the major, source of employment for the Singapore population and a source of income for the Singapore merchants. As a result, Lee Kuan Yew came sniffing around the bases to have a look at the assets he would inherit, which he could then somehow convert into civilian enterprises that would enable the island's economy to survive. Changi was one such base that Mr. Lee came to inspect, and the Electronics Squadron building was on his itinerary. We were instructed to treat him with the utmost respect and come to attention if he passed near our location, which he did in my case. I gave it the old "Officer present" treatment we had been taught in basic training. Mr. Lee looked over at me when I did this and nodded towards me in acknowledgement. And that's my claim to fame, even if it is somewhat reflected.

Mick, the SAC mentioned above, was detailed to help me with the generator testing, although we did other kinds of testing as well. Mick was easy to get along with, but I felt sad for him. He was divorced and apparently rudderless in his personal life. Unfortunately, he had a fondness for the booze and the bar girls, generally in that order. Consequently, he suffered with a chronic case of gonorrhoea and was a frequent visitor to the Station Sick Quarters. He was very open about discussing his condition and told me that the Sick Quarters staff usually threatened him with the "upside down umbrella" treatment if he kept returning there. This, he said was a small, slim instrument pushed up into the urethra and, when inserted far enough, was then opened like an umbrella and dragged back out, bringing "stuff" with it. Yuk! However, I don't believe this supposed treatment for the disease really existed, but the threat was used as a kind of "bogeyman" in an attempt to scare Mick into exercising more restraint in consorting with the local professional ladies.

Another of our E&I Section airmen was a small but sturdy Scot. A rough and ready type of person who, I imagine, must have been a drill instructor's worst nightmare during his square-bashing days because he was about as far as you could get from being the spit & polish type. He was married and lived out, and used to roll in late to work, looking dishevelled as though he had been on an all-night binge. His KD – he wore the standard issue – certainly had the appearance of having been slept in all night. And this was every day, not just on rare occasions. Any criticism directed at him was just met with a smirk to the point where we NCOs just let him be as long as his work performance was acceptable. Jock, for want of a better name, was definitely a free-spirit and you couldn't help but like him, even though his lifestyle was as rough as his appearance. I remember one Saturday, when a small group of us had to work for some long-forgotten reason – usually, we didn't work during the weekends. At lunchtime that day, Jock decided to go into Changi Village to get something to eat. A little later, he returned with a filled *roti* – a round, flat pancake-like piece of flatbread similar to an Indian chapati or a Mexican tortilla that was wrapped around some kind of meat filling. He had bought it from one of the streetside food vendor stalls in the village, from which most of us would never eat anything because of the questionable hygiene. Not only that, but he also brought back some hot tea, or maybe it was coffee, which in itself was okay, but the drink was in a small tin can that had once contained something else, possibly condensed milk. It was common to see local people carrying around hot drinks in this manner that they too had purchased from street vendors, but never RAF personnel. The still-attached top of the tin-can, that had been opened with a tin opener, was pierced in the middle and a thin bamboo "string" threaded through to form a long, looped carrying handle that allowed the tin-can to be dangled from the hand, so as to avoid having to be in direct contact with the hot metal. Jock brought his *roti* and tin can of hot beverage back to the section and proceeded to bend the lid back to form a handle just like the locals did, and then drank the contents and wolfed down the *roti*. I had the feeling that he did it just to see the horrified look on everyone's faces, but that was Jock.

* * *

But even if the day-to-day work was rather ho-hum, the good thing about the section was the camaraderie that existed between us, or at least the married contingent. Being married and "accompanied" (the term being accompanied by one's wife during an overseas tour) was financially beneficial. We were paid a generous overseas allowance as well as a marriage allowance and even an allowance to cover the cost of hiring an amah. This was understandably resented by those who were single or unaccompanied for some reason. They even had a derogatory nickname for us – Scalies. I'm not sure of the source of the word, but suspect it was derived from the "pay scales" that were used to compute our pay. To add to our comparatively bounteous income, we also were entitled to a monthly ration of two dozen cans of Tiger Beer from the NAAFI, at a heavily discounted price. This generous allowance of beer helped to fuel many of our social gatherings, of which there were many. Indeed, Pam and I enjoyed a great social life together with the other members of the Electrical Section. Nowadays, because of my advanced age, I am unable to recall the names of most of them, although I do remember Dave Thornley, but that's because he and I had both been posted not only to the same station three times in a row, (not counting my short stint at Labuan), but to the same Section. We were both on Kestrel Squadron at RAF West Raynham from 1964 until 1966. Then, when the squadron was disbanded, we both arrived in the Electrical Bay at RAF Scampton together. From there, I was posted to Labuan, but when I got transferred to Changi, guess who was there in the E&I Section to welcome me. Of the others, I recall some first names that still lurk within the old grey matter. There was Frank, an SAC, Ray, a J/T I think, Glen, a corporal and although I can't remember her Ground Electrician husband's name, there was Ethel who hailed from my native Northern Ireland. Ethel certainly wasn't a frail, shrinking violet sort of a woman, she had the kind of build that would have made a brick outhouse envious. She had an unusable hand that may have been from an accident or birth defect, I can't remember which, but it didn't affect her great sense of humour. There were many more friends who were also co-workers than those few mentioned, but their names completely elude me after all this time.

Parties at each other's residences were a common occurrence. The ladies took full advantage of the inexpensive dress makers that abounded in Singapore and usually showed up in beautiful outfits. Those couples with young children didn't have to find someone to baby-sit, as would have been the case back home. Everyone employed an amah, which for those blessed with children, already provided them with a full-time baby-sitter. We also joined up with the others for evenings at various entertainment venues, such as the Ocean Park Hotel that had an outside stage featuring excellent bands and singers. I still remember one South Korean female duo that sang songs in English although I had the sneaking suspicion they didn't know or understand the words they were singing. One song, "Love Is a Many Splendored Thing," was sung beautifully, except that the words came out as "Ruvv is a merry sprendor sing."

All dressed up with somewhere to go!

Most weekends, several of us along with our wives, and the children of those who had them, gathered around the enormous swimming pool at the Britannia Club on Beach Road. The club was directly opposite the famous Raffles Hotel. There we lazed in the sun, having an occasional dip in the pool to cool off, but most of the time just socializing while drinking Cokes, at least the ladies drank them, we lads were more inclined to partake of a Tiger or two.

Although Raffles was nearby, I now regret that I never ventured into this famed hotel that boasted the famous 'Long Bar.'

But, David Holgate, who was stationed in Singapore at around the same time, remembers that the room containing the Long Bar was approximately 40 metres long and 20 – 25 metres wide. The bar itself was approximately 30 metres long. The room was furnished with rattan tables and chairs, while several ceiling fans spun lazily to circulate the air. The adjoining tropical garden was home to several cabins that were named after famous guests such as Somerset Maugham.

The famous Raffles hotel in 1968. Taken from the Britannia Club on the opposite side of Nichol Highway.
(From personal photo library)

* * *

Mohammed bin Saad, one of the locally employed men who worked at the dirty job of stripping down and servicing the aircraft generators, alternators, and other rotating electrical equipment, invited all members of the Section to his son's wedding. He was a small, cheerful Malay man who normally went by the name of Saad and lived in the local Kampong Changi. On the appointed evening, we all turned up at the kampong suitably dressed to attend the wedding, which in

Singapore consisted of a long-sleeved shirt and tie with a smart pair of trousers. The ladies, of course, had all been in consultation with their dressmakers and came all dolled up in the finest couture and perfect hairdos. It was a wedding after all, so what a great reason to go a little bit beyond the ordinary. And a good thing it was too. It was as if the ladies had anticipated that and, in addition to the bride and groom, who were the main attraction, our group would also feature as secondary attractions that evening.

We had anticipated mingling with the people of the kampong and other local wedding guests, so it was surprising to realize that this was a reception for outside guests only and not the kampong people. A few tables had been set up in an open area in the middle of the kampong with place settings for the guests. We of the E&I Section were ushered to our own table, while other guests were seated at a neighbouring table.

Everything about a Malayan wedding and its preliminaries is very formal, beginning as far back as the betrothal and the engagement, with several steps between those and the actual wedding ceremony. The reception is the finale which doesn't necessarily take place on the same day as the wedding itself. But, for the reception, the groom and his bride are King and Queen for the day and sit on a pair of thrones and are the focal point of the reception. It was an honour for us to be invited, but there was also a not-so-subtle reason for our presence there. The good thing was that we didn't need to go shopping for a wedding present that would be acceptable to a happy couple in the West. Instead, the traditional wedding gift for a Malay bride and groom was good old-fashioned cash. We all went to the wedding suitably prepared.

We took our places at the table, noticing that the inhabitants of the kampong, mostly women and children, stood around in the shadows watching all of us intently, while smiling and chattering to each other. Drinks were served, but nothing alcoholic. Malays are mostly Muslim for whom alcohol is forbidden, so the drinks were either soft drinks or just plain water poured for us by well-dressed men acting as waiters.

     When everyone had been seated, the happy couple emerged from one of the houses adjoining the reception area. They were both dressed in traditional Malay clothing, but instead of being fashioned from everyday material, the clothing was all of fine silk brocade. A double throne-like structure had been set up on a dais near the tables and on which the couple sat side by side facing the guests. Having been pre-advised, we had all come armed with banknotes of suitable denominations as our gifts. Something in the order of twenty Singapore dollars. At a given cue, a female guest from the other table approached the happy couple and, picking up a small safety-pin from a small dish on a table near the throne, proceeded to pin a banknote on to the bride's silk brocade costume. The donor then returned to her place at her table, upon which one of the male guests made his way out to the happy couple and repeated the action, but he pinned the money on to the groom's outfit. We had thus been educated on the proper procedure and, when everyone seated at the other table had made their pilgrimage, we all took our turn in pinning our gifts to the couple's clothing, receiving a pleasantly polite 'thank you' in return.

The clothing worn by this couple is similar to that worn by the bride and groom at the wedding we attended.

When all the last guests had donated their wedding gifts, it was time for the feast. Plates of Malay curry were set before us and, in the centre of the table, a selection of small dishes containing a variety of condiments, some recognizable as slices of banana and other cut up fruit as well as raisins, but other items were not so obvious. All of these were available to mix in with the curry, together with the ample quantity of rice that was provided.

Malay curry is very spicy, and one forkful leaves the average British diner's mouth feeling as though it's on fire. The organizers obviously knew this because we were assured several times that this was a mild curry. I have always enjoyed a good curry and could tolerate spicy hot Indian curries such as Madras and Vindaloo dishes, but I was pleased that we didn't get the full-strength kampong variety of this particular Malay curry because the "mild" version easily beat every Madras or Vindaloo that I had ever sampled for spiciness. The thing about any spicy meal is that once the mouth becomes, shall we say acclimatised, it becomes easier to eat, so after a few mouthfuls, I was enjoying it and didn't think too much about the curry stew's contents. That state of blissful ignorance lasted for most of the meal and would have continued until the end if Ethel, our Northern Irish friend, hadn't leaned across the table and, with an impish smile playing around her lips, said to me in a conspiratorial tone of voice, "That was a nice bit of goat, don't you think, Brian?"

Part of our E&I Section contingent at the Malayan wedding. Ethel is the woman on the right in the dark dress and her husband is on the extreme right. The bride and groom are socializing with the table behind ours and the kampong spectators can be seen at the top left of the photo.

The meat content of the curry was certainly not chicken and, since Singapore does not have any cattle, all beef is imported and therefore relatively expensive. Nor are there any sheep, the nearest probably being somewhere in Australia, but there are plenty of goats on the island that are raised by the Malay population. I hadn't thought of it up to that moment, but Ethel's sly comment now made me realize what we all had been eating. I just had to laugh, it was so funny the way she said it, besides, goat probably tastes very much like mutton, not that there was any perceptible flavour due to the dish's extreme spiciness, so no one was any the worse off.

***

It wasn't "social life with friends" all the time, though. Pam and I went out by ourselves to restaurants and enjoyed discovering other parts of Singapore and the nearby Malay Peninsula. I have already mentioned the Coq d'Or restaurant, but there were other good restaurants, especially on Orchard Road, where there were many posh hotels and the nice restaurants that spring up around such establishments.

We went sight-seeing to such places as the Botanical Gardens and to the more famous Tiger Balm Garden, which portrayed scenes from Chinese mythology in the form of garishly decorated statuary. The garden was financed by the profits from Tiger Balm, a kind of heal-all ointment similar to Vicks VapoRub®.

* * *

Seeing off the Moonlighter was also one of our favourite evening pastimes. "What's the Moonlighter?" you're probably thinking right now. Okay, let me explain – the "Moonlighter" was featured in an advert placed by BOAC in the local *Straits Times* newspaper to promote its daily, or I should say nightly, Super VC10 service from Singapore to London. This was back when there were two nationalized airlines: British European Airways otherwise known as BEA, and BOAC the British Overseas Airways Corporation. Although the VC10 arrived at Paya Lebar airport every afternoon, it didn't depart on its return flight to Heathrow until 11:30 pm. This late-night departure apparently inspired someone at BOAC to come up with the brilliant and romantic sounding "Moonlighter" tag.

For our part, although Singapore was a plum posting, we were always nostalgic for the homeland, and anything connected with it, so when we saw the Moonlighter advert in the Straits Times, we knew that it was something we had to see.

On our first visit to see it, we made our way to the "waving gallery" that was a feature of many airports in less troubled times. I had waited there to watch the arrival of the British Eagle Britannia that brought Pam, when she came to join me, and waved to her when she came down the steps from the aircraft. (That was another relic of the past – there were no airbridges back then. A moveable stairway was wheeled up to the aircraft to enable passengers and crew to board or disembark from an aircraft).

The waving gallery was really an open-air balcony associated with the airport lounge bar and featured a few tables and chairs where we were able sit and order drinks. Down below, not a stone's throw away, aircraft belonging to different airlines continuously arrived and departed – Pan Am Boeing 707s, Garuda (Indonesian) DC8s and numerous others. The aircraft were marshalled in to form a flightline that was perpendicular to the terminal. At the end of the line and nearest to the waving gallery sat the BOAC VC10, resplendent in its livery. The famous BOAC "Speedbird" adorned the dark blue tailfin and, on a similarly dark blue coloured horizontal stripe that ran the length of the fuselage, the legend "BOAC" was proudly displayed in large letters just behind the cockpit. What made this livery stand out above all others, though, was that both the Speedbird symbol and the BOAC lettering were both applied in reflective gold. The proud, regal appearance that its livery conferred on the VC10 made it to stand out amongst the other airliners as a swan would appear amongst a gaggle of geese.

After that first visit, it became a regular thing for us to go out to the airport and enjoy a drink in the cool of the evening while watching all the different airliners come and go. The highlight of the night was when the Moonlighter passengers boarded, and then when it started up and taxied out to the runway. I believe there was a spotlight shining on the Speedbird symbol as the aircraft rolled down the runway on its take-off run, a wonderful sight to behold indeed. We only wished that we were on it.

* * *

In September of 1967, I took a week's leave so that Pam and I could spend some time exploring the whole island, and even going further afield by crossing the causeway connecting Singapore island to the Malayan Peninsula. Because we didn't own any transport, I rented an Austin Mini from the local Hertz rent-a-car, and off we set.

For the first few days, we went in different directions to see as much of Singapore and its attractions as possible, which we covered in a few days. Then, when we couldn't think of anywhere that we had missed, we set off early one day and drove up to the north side of the island, where the causeway joins up with Johore Bahru, the nearest point on the Malaysian side. There was a queue at the Customs post to get across where each car was inspected by Singapore officials before being allowed to cross over. One of the things they were on the lookout for was to see how much petrol Singapore licensed cars had in the tank. Petrol in Singapore was quite a bit more expensive than on the Malaysian side because of added taxes, so the government had decreed that any Singapore vehicle crossing the causeway must have at least three quarters of a tankful. There was even a traffic sign that showed a diagram of a car's petrol gauge with the needle at the three-quarter point together with a written directive to top up. We were well aware of this law, because it was fairly new and had had lots of publicity, so I had made sure we had enough fuel in the tank.

Once we had crossed over into Malaysia, it was obvious that we were in a different country. The hustle and bustle of Singapore was left behind as we found ourselves in a quiet, rural environment. Our vague destination was a bay on the east coast that friends had referred to as Jason's Bay.

Most of the countryside was given over to plantations of one kind or another. Pineapples grew on one large patch of land. We had never in our lives seen how pineapples grow, and possibly imagined that they grew on trees like Granny Smith apples. We were therefore surprised to see that each pineapple is at the centre of a large plant with spiky leaves, that grows from the ground up and that the pineapple itself grows in an upright direction from its mother plant. The end of the pineapple that has the spiky leaves is actually the bottom, not the top, although they are usually portrayed as though the leafy end is the top.

Further along, we came upon a rubber tree plantation. I had remembered learning about this from geography lessons during my schooldays, about how a v-shaped cut was made in the tree bark and a small cup placed at the low point of the vee to catch the raw rubber as it oozed out of the bark, and was curious to see this in real life, so to speak. Treading carefully, I went to the nearest tree and sure enough, it was just like I had been told at school. A little metal spout was impaled into the tree at the low point of the vee and a small cup placed under it. The white rubber sap had collected in the bottom of the cup and was still in liquid form when I tested it by dipping the tip of my index finger into it. Meanwhile, I was being attacked by some very vicious mosquitoes. These weren't the Singapore kind of mosquito that sneaked around looking for an opportunity to land somewhere on the body to bite. No, these little buggers came straight at me, proboscis out and at the ready to jab into wherever they landed. They looked different as well – dark, a little larger and with prominent stripes on their long, rear legs. Smacking hard at them as they made their landing, I beat a hasty retreat back to the car and slammed the door to escape the onslaught.

Examing the contents of the cup that collects the raw rubber from an incision in the rubber tree bark.

Eventually, we arrived at Jason's Bay, but by this time, the sun had disappeared behind ominously heavy clouds, and it appeared as though it had already rained there. Nevertheless, we got out of the car to explore our surroundings and were confronted by a wide bay rimmed by a broad, sandy beach that seemed to stretch for miles and was completely deserted. We walked along it for a while as hundreds of small sand crabs scuttled ahead of us, each disappearing down its little hole in the sand as we approached. Soon, we took our shoes off and paddled in the warm, shallow water along its edge. The beach was still wet from the rain that had preceded our arrival, and it was now late in the afternoon, so we didn't stay too long before setting off for the Johore Bahru causeway and a return to Singapore.

That was our first, but not our last visit to Malaysia. On another occasion, we travelled to the western side of the peninsula, with a spectacular waterfall as our destination. Our last was a holiday in Penang, but more about that later.

Chapter 13: West meets East

Living in Singapore was like experiencing three Asian countries simultaneously: China, Malaysia, and India.

The Chinese people living in Singapore were typically referred to as Overseas Chinese, most of whom weren't particularly big fans of Communist China. They were, by far, the largest ethnic group, eclipsing the Malay people who were the original inhabitants of not just Singapore, but the entire Malay Peninsula of which Singapore was an offshore island, (although attached to the peninsula by a causeway), and the neighbouring Indonesian archipelago. The smallest major ethnic group was Indian, who were further subdivided variously into Hindus, Sikhs, and Tamils. The British and Commonwealth military presence formed a smaller but important fourth group.

The majority of the Commonwealth representatives was British – Royal Air Force, Royal Navy and British Army. The minority consisted of Australians and New Zealanders. As an overall group, we were children of Western culture with customs and traditions very much different to those of the permanent inhabitants of the city state of Singapore.

Just being there with the temperature, the humidity, the wildlife, both insect and otherwise, the racial mix of the population and the everyday sights and sounds of the Far East was a cultural experience in its own right, but our first memorable encounter with the different customs was Chinese New Year. This event isn't a fixed calendar date as it is with our own New Year's Day on the 1st of January each year. Rather, it is determined by the lunar cycle and falls between 21st of January and the 20th of February, depending on when the second new moon following the winter solstice appears in the sky. In 1967, the first year that Pam and I experienced it, was the 9th of February, and was named the Year of the Goat.

At midnight that night, we sat expectantly on the balcony of our flat. Earlier, we had noticed the long strings of firecrackers dangling from poles outside several of the other flats. When the magic hour struck, the strings were lit off from the bottom and the noise was deafening. It was surprising how much of a bang those little crackers made individually, and when several were going off at the same time, it got very noisy and continued as the detonations worked their way up the strings. Smoke and small shreds of paper from the exploding bodies of the crackers were everywhere. After half an hour, we had had enough, but not our Chinese neighbours. Firecrackers were being let off just about all night, making it difficult to get to sleep when bedtime came around. So much for New Year's night, or so we thought, not realizing that the celebration, and firecrackers, continued for a whole two weeks, so it was more of the same for the next twelve nights, although a little less each night. Except, on the last night, all hell broke loose again as more and more firecrackers were let off. The next year, we knew what to expect, but that first Chinese New Year was an eye opener – literally!

***

One day, we heard a commotion out on Amber Road, the street between Rose Garden and the neighbouring kampong, that brought us to the rear balcony to see what was going on. We were just in time to see what looked like a lot of small pieces of paper tossed up into the air, although the pieces could have been flower petals. We then noticed what looked like a parade float, but quickly realized it was the Chinese equivalent of a funeral hearse. Grabbing my camera, I rushed over to get some photos, which are included below. The recently deceased must have been a person of some importance, because the funeral procession included a small marching band and a large procession of mourners, all of whom were dressed in white – the Chinese mourning colour that's equivalent to our mourning black. The parade was far from quiet, thanks to the band that played a noisy cacophony of drums, trumpets, clarinets, and trombones.

WEST MEETS EAST 135

The "Hearse"

The "Band"

The "Mourners"

Another Chinese custom – one that is associated with ancestor worship, seemed odd to my Western mind. When we lived at Cheviot Hill, it was necessary to walk a short distance to the main road to be able to hail a pick-up taxi. On the way, I passed one particular home that, for several days, had an elaborate table covered with a red tablecloth set up on its front patio. The table was festooned with a number of dishes containing food and different kinds of fruit. Several smouldering joss sticks completed the arrangement, their fragrant smoke filling the air. So far, you might think there's nothing too odd about that, but seated on a chair at the table and facing out into the street was the effigy of a man dressed in what we would consider to be normal clothing, including a hat. It wasn't difficult to realize that this was homage to a deceased relative, perhaps a father or grandfather. On one occasion, a woman stood in front of the table, facing the effigy where she placed freshly lit joss-sticks and then bowed several times towards the man with her hands placed together as though in prayer.

***

Chinese street operas called *wayangs* began making their appearance at a certain time of the year. Only a stone-deaf person could be unaware of one of these when it was performing in the neighbourhood because of the loud caterwauling that passed for singing, the gongs and the discordant music played on traditional Chinese stringed instruments. Elaborate stages were set up on street corners on which the *wayangs* were performed and around which spectators gathered to watch. It was a spectacle to behold – actors in colourful, ornate, flowing robes and head-dresses, with exaggerated facial makeup. The costumes always appeared to have long, white, flowing sleeves that extended far beyond the performers hands and these were waved around dramatically by whichever character was singing at any given time. It was interesting to watch, but the singing and music made it difficult to withstand for very long, so we usually had a quick look before moving on far enough to be well out of earshot.

Attribution: Zoharby, CC BY-SA 3.0
<https://creativecommons.org/licenses/by-sa/3.0>, via Wikimedia Commons

***

Sometimes, Pam and I would catch a bus to Bedok Junction, where there was a small beach on which we could spend an afternoon, sunbathing and swimming. The buses on this local service were ramshackle, third-world vintage vehicles, but it was inexpensive and convenient because there was a bus stop right outside Rose Garden and the trip wasn't very long. Getting on the bus was an experience because the locals seemed to have no concept of queuing – it was every man and woman for themselves. Once on board, elderly Chinese would slap the seat three or four times before sitting down. We were informed that this was to drive out any evil spirits that may have been hitching a ride or had been left by the previous seat occupant.

***

The strangest custom we witnessed wasn't Chinese or Malay, but Indian. It was not so much a custom as a Hindu religious event or festival named *Thaipusam* during which Hindu devotees pushed metal skewers all the way through their cheeks, from one side of the face to the other and some even had a second skewer pushed through the top and bottom lips, passing through their tongue. Some also had what looked like two rows of fishhooks that were hooked all the way through the skin of their upper back and from which dangled small fruit that looked like limes or figs. The devotees walked in a procession from one temple to another carrying an ornate wooden structure across their shoulders.

We had heard about this festival, which was also a public holiday in Singapore, and learned that the temple welcomed all comers to witness the ritual, so we decided to attend. The atmosphere in the crowded temple from where the procession would start, was heady. Mesmerizing Indian music played continuously as the participants, who seemed to be in a trance-like state, chanted along with it. That, together with the smell of incense lent an almost psychedelic feeling that enwrapped us. The devotees were all gathered in a courtyard within the temple confines and we, together with the other onlookers, most of whom were Indian, stood on the wide steps that led down into the courtyard. Ceremonies had already been held from the early morning hours to place the skewers and fishhooks as well as place the structures, known as *kavadis*, on the shoulders of the participants. All of them were bare from the waist up and covered in what looked like a grey ash, which had also been applied to their faces. Although the skewers and hooks were definitely piercing all the way through the skin, there was absolutely no blood seeping from the wounds. Moreover, the participants were jigging around while they chanted, and I couldn't help noticing how the little limes or figs bobbed around on the hooks from which they dangled. As time passed, the individuals joined the procession as it left the temple, and we watched until the last one had gone before leaving ourselves. We didn't follow them to the other temple, which was a few miles away, but could see them jigging around as the proceeded in that direction. This was probably the most bizarre thing we ever witnessed in our entire lives, let alone in Singapore.

Devotees with piercings through their mouths and other parts of the body. Although we didn't personally see any women participating in the procession, this photo shows at least four, although they do not appear to have piercings.
Photo credit: Wikipedia: https://en.wikipedia.org/wiki/Thaipusam

***

Weekly night-time street markets were popular both with the Singaporeans and we of the British and Commonwealth Forces. They were known by the Malay name *pasar malam*, meaning "night market," (although the noun comes first in the Malay language – *pasar* is the word for market). Certain areas held their markets on a specific night of the week and on these nights, stalls would be set up along a given street in the area. They weren't unlike the weekly open-air markets back in the homeland, except that they were held at night, when the temperature was more tolerable. There was an air of romanticism about them because lighting was mostly by the soft glow of Tilley lamps on many of the stalls although some had fluorescent lighting that was probably powered from a nearby residence. The markets sold all manner of goods such as clothing, housewares, craftwork, paintings, pirated music tapes, and a long list of miscellaneous offerings. Price negotiation was the order of business, so a person needed to be fairly skilled at that practice, although anyone who had been in Singapore for a reasonable time was well used to this method of purchasing. Some things were good, but in reality, most of it was shoddy, although the vendors tried to pass their wares off as good quality. I recall one stall owner who sold dinner sets telling us that a certain set was "Maru-taki." I laughed at this and commented that it wasn't Noritake, which is the brand name of an excellent quality Japanese chinaware, (pronounced Norry-tacky). The good-natured vendor laughed as well, while telling me that Maru-taki was "the brother of Noritake." We wished him well and moved on to other stalls.

***

I wouldn't want to finish this chapter without mentioning the Durian fruit, which is unknown to most Westerners, and with good reason. This yellow, watermelon-sized fruit with a thick, thorny outer rind, is considered to be a great delicacy by the people of Southeast Asia. They love the aroma and its flavour so much that when Durian comes into season, special stalls appear everywhere to sell the fruit. Stallholders keep on hand a small brush shaped like an old-fashioned shaving brush, except that the "bristles" are made of bamboo strips and are stiff. I have seen customers using this kind of "brush" to repeatedly stab the rind, creating multiple small punctures, and then putting their noses close to the stabbed area to deeply inhale the odour. Presumably, the stronger the smell, the more desirable the Durian.

But for some strange reason, the olfactory senses of those of us from the Western World seem to be wired differently from those of our Southeast Asian cousins, because to me and to everyone else with whom I was acquainted, the Durian emits the most disgusting, repulsive smell imaginable, which spreads over a large area. A travel writer named Richard Sterling describes it best by what he has written, "…its odour is best described as pig-excrement, turpentine and onions, garnished with a gym sock. It can be smelled from yards away. Despite its great local popularity, the raw fruit is forbidden from some establishments such as hotels, subways, and airports, including public transportation in Southeast Asia."

Chapter 14: Lessons Learned

When I joined the RAF as a Boy Entrant, I was given the option of signing on for either 12 years, or for 10 years and 2 in the Reserve. As a fifteen-year-old boy, both of those seemed like a lifetime, so I chose the lesser of the two, the "engagement" beginning from the date of my 18th birthday. We all experience the phenomena that time speeds up as we age, so that in 1968 I sensed that demob was unexpectedly imminent the following year. Having no intention of staying in the Service, my thoughts turned to what I would do in "civvy street." I didn't have a single civilian qualification, unless we count passing the 11+ when I was 12 years old. Up to now, it hadn't mattered in the RAF, having made it to corporal by passing all the necessary trade tests. Would that carry much weight in the outside world? I doubted it, but I had a bit of time, so decided to consult with the Education Section, my thought being to obtain a few 'O' Level GCEs (General Certificates of Education, Ordinary Level).

The Education Officer listened patiently when I asked if I could take the 'O' Levels in Maths, English, and Physics. He then looked up my RAF education records, observing that my only RAF academic qualification was the RAF Education Test Part I, which I had taken and passed during my Boy Entrant training. Before he would sanction me to attend any GCE classes, he said I would need to take and pass the RAF Education Test Part II, so I enrolled in those three classes.

I wasn't too worried about the English subject because I had always found it easy, although I did learn some new things. One that I remember from that time was what the teaching officer referred to as a Precis, which was new to me. The idea was, that before writing an essay, write down ten sentences that summarized the content of the essay and flesh out the essay around those ten thoughts.

Maths, however, was a different kettle of fish. It had been a long time since I sat in a classroom and, as a result, my expertise in the subject was extremely limited. That old saying, 'use it or lose it' isn't just empty words. Besides, I had never gone beyond basic algebra. The first maths class was therefore a gigantic embarrassment when it became obvious how little I knew or remembered. Looking around for some way to catch up, I visited a bookstore and found a book titled "Teach Yourself Algebra." Leafing through it, I could see that it could possibly provide me with the lifeline I needed to be able to pass the education test. I bought the book and, every night for the next few weeks, I worked through it, reading the text, and working the examples. The book also came with an unexpected bonus – although it was supposedly devoted to algebra, there was a later chapter that dealt with logarithms. This was a subject of which I was completely ignorant, never having been taught it, although I had heard the word bandied about. So, I got working on that, and soon achieved a good level of competency in the subject. It all helped, giving me the confidence and basic knowledge to continue with the maths class and eventually pass the test. Incidentally, an updated version of the book is still around and can be found on book-selling websites – and I still have my original copy, which came in useful in helping one of my grandchildren to get a better grasp of algebra.

Physics was much more interesting and enjoyable, the teacher being a down to earth, no-airs-and-graces engineering officer. At one point, I approached him privately, with some trepidation, to ask how a person could become an engineer. Of course, I was referring to myself and hoped he wouldn't think it a stupid question. He didn't think that, but instead advised me that I would at least need to have a Higher National Certificate in engineering – generally referred to as an HNC. At the time, that seemed like a bridge too far; after all, I didn't even have a bloody GCE 'O' Level to my name. Little did I know then that, in time, I would achieve what had then seemed to be such an unreachable goal, but I'm away ahead of the narrative here, so I'll get back into the moment.

With the RAF Education Test successfully passed, I now turned my sights on the GCE and enrolled in the English Language and Maths classes. I had decided not to take the Physics because I thought the two other subjects were the most important and I wanted to concentrate on them.

Again, the English subject came easy to me, but to learn the Maths in such a manner as to pass the exam was a bit of a challenge. I remember that one of the things the Education Officer teaching the class harped on about was that those of us taking it needed to be able to prove the Pythagoras Theorem because it was usually a standard question on the exam paper. At first, I didn't understand why I would need to prove it. After all, it was fairly obvious that *"the square on the hypotenuse equalled the sum of the squares on the other two sides."* All you had to do was draw a 3-4-5 triangle and square the sides – $3^2 = 9$, $4^2 = 16$ and $5^2 = 25$. And so, $9 + 16 = 25$ of which the square root is 5, so like I said, it's obvious. But no, there is a convoluted formal proof that had to be learned step by step. It took quite a few practices to be able to remember all the steps and work through them to come to the final statement that indeed proved the theorem.

In June 1968, when I sat for both exams, sure enough, the Pythagoras proof question came up on the Maths paper but having practiced it often enough to be able to do it in my sleep, I got it down on the answer paper with enough time left to be able to finish all of the other questions. Time was critical because, like most exams, there was a set time and if you spent too much time on one question, it could rob you of the time needed to finish all the questions, which was a good way of failing to pass, but I finished on time and passed both exams.

***

Another type of lesson needed to be learned, but it had nothing to do with the Education Section. Although the RAF used the most modern technology for its air war capability, ground defence was still using First World War vintage weaponry in the form of the Lee Enfield .303 rifle on which we had all been trained. Finally moving into the Twentieth Century in that regard, the RAF together with the other Services, adopted the Belgian FN rifle, otherwise known as the NATO rifle, because it was supposed to be standard throughout all NATO forces, (although the Americans never adopted it).

The rifle was automatic in that having cocked it to chamber the first round, the subsequent rounds were loaded into the firing chamber automatically by a mechanism operated by the gas pressure released from the firing of the first cartridge. As such, the weapon was referred to by the RAF Regiment as the SLR – self-loading rifle. The good news was that when the rifle was fired, its self-loading mechanism absorbed the nasty "kick" that we suffered when firing the Lee Enfield .303.

Ground defence training on the rifle was organized by the RAF Regiment and everyone in the ranks was detailed to attend one-day training classes. When it was my day to attend the class, the Regiment instructor spent the morning showing us how it all worked and how to calibrate the backsight to line up with the foresight so that it would be exactly on the target. The calibration exercise meant working in two-man teams. One man aimed the rifle at a small white card held by the other man, who had taken up position a specified distance away, and was lying on the ground, facing towards the aimed rifle. There was a cross marked on the card with a small hole in its centre. The cross was the aiming point, and so the man holding the card peered through the hole when his fellow team member aimed the rifle at the card with the centre of the cross in the centre of his sights. The man peering through the hole was supposed to see the dark hole of open muzzle exactly centred as though a round, if fired, would hit him directly in the eye, but most times he would see only a portion of the muzzle exit. The job then was to inform the aimer of the discrepancy and have him adjust the backsight until the muzzle was exactly centred on the card-holder's eye.

The afternoon was dedicated to live firing on the range. After learning all about the SLR, I was looking forward to some shooting minus the painful kickback that was part and parcel of shooting with the Lee Enfield, but you win some and you lose some. Lying in the prone firing position, I loaded five rimless rounds, as we had been taught and waited for the order to fire. When it came, I took aim at the bullseye on the target and gently squeezed the trigger. I seem to recall from the morning session that the trigger didn't have a "second pressure" like the Lee Enfield, there was only one pressure, so I kept squeezing until the action fired. As expected, there was no kick, but what I didn't expect was the sudden pain and deafness in my right ear. Of course, in those days, we weren't provided with ear protection. After firing all five rounds, I got up and left the rifle where it was, ready for the next victim. My ear still hurt badly, and continued to hurt for the next few days, although the hearing in that ear gradually returned, but it never regained its former quality, even to this day.

As a side note, several years later, in civilian life, I had to undergo a medical examination for a job I was about to take in Saudi Arabia. The company that was hiring me sent me to a doctor in Harley Street for the exam, one part of which was a hearing test. Afterwards, the doctor went over the results of the exam with me, all of which were satisfactory. He actually pronounced me "fighting fit," however, when he came to the hearing test, he asked me if I had ever fired the NATO rifle. I was surprised at the question, but answered yes, that I had. He then said my answer confirmed his suspicions because the hearing test graph showed that, at a one particular frequency, I had marked hearing loss. The doctor then went on to say that he had seen this many times before, and nearly always with former servicemen who had fired the NATO rifle. Oddly enough, I had been given a hearing test during my RAF release medical during which it was noted as being "normal." Which finding should I believe? An easy question to answer – I'm inclined to believe the Harley Street doctor's findings rather than those of the RAF.

Chapter 15: Penang

Days to do were getting few, as National Service men used to say when their two-year compulsory service was nearly at an end. Usually, they knew how many days they had left, almost to the hour, and would gladly inform anyone who inquired of that number and then add, "…and an early breakfast!" Meaning they didn't intend to be hanging around on the day they regained their civilian status. In my case, it just meant that the end of my overseas tour was rapidly approaching – but there would be no "early breakfast." However, Pam and I felt the urge to go away on holiday. We had heard about Penang, and that there was a NAAFI Holiday Camp there; can you imagine a Butlin's style holiday camp run by that often-maligned organization? From what I had heard, it wasn't bad, even if there were no Red Coats to organize activities and, on reflection, that was probably a good thing. Anyway, I put in for a leave pass and when it was granted, we made a reservation at the holiday camp through the Changi NAAFI, and booked a flight on Malaysia Singapore Airlines, or MSA as it was known then.

On the appointed day, we took a taxi to Paya Lebar airport and boarded a MSA de Havilland Comet 4C. This was the first time I had flown in a pure jet aircraft, even though I had mostly worked plenty of RAF jets up to that point, so I was looking forward to the experience and the prospect of chalking up another life milestone. The flight was enjoyable and uneventful, even though it sounded as though there to be a rough bearing in one of the engines, but this being my first time, I thought maybe it was typical. Having logged many hours in passenger jets in later life, I can honestly say that I have never heard a similar groaning sound during any subsequent flights, so maybe there was something to be worried about – but we arrived safely in Penang, which qualifies as a happy ending.

Penang turned out to be a wonderful place to spend a holiday. There was so much to do. The camp itself was fairly basic, but the staff excelled themselves in making it a great experience, even though they didn't wear red coats. There weren't too many guests, in fact, I can only remember one other couple being there, with whom we soon made friends. The camp had a supply of fishing rods, so we went fishing for catfish on one side of the property where the sea washed up against the rock wall that kept it at bay (no pun intended). The fish were easy to catch and land, but the supervising staff member advised caution because of the wickedly barbed dorsal and lateral spines that floppy-looking outer sheaths disguised as harmless. Sure enough, when I landed my first and bashed it with one of my flip-flops, the spine easily penetrated the rubber sole all the way through. Fortunately, I had used the flip-flop like a fly swatter and wasn't wearing it on my foot.

The camp also owned a speed boat in which another staff member would take us out for a spin. One day, we noticed a series of Chinese junks sailing out of the local harbour, so the four of us (I can't remember our friends' names) asked the speedboat pilot to take us out for some photo opportunities.

Outside of the camp, there was plenty to do. We went on a guided tour of Penang, arranged through the camp staff. Penang has a famous snake temple that's the home of an overwhelming number of deadly vipers that are reputedly subdued by the incense. So, it was one of the stops on the tour. Some of our fellow tourists, who were brave enough, allowed themselves to have a snake placed on their shoulder – neither of us volunteered. I noticed, though, that all the snakes that were being handled, and even those lying around on the altar and elsewhere, had an almost inconspicuous red spot on their head. Later, I found out that the snakes were de-venomed, although they still had their fangs, so it seemed that the red mark was to let the handlers know which snakes were safe to handle. It was still an awesome experience to be up close to and be surrounded by so many of the supposedly deadly pit vipers.

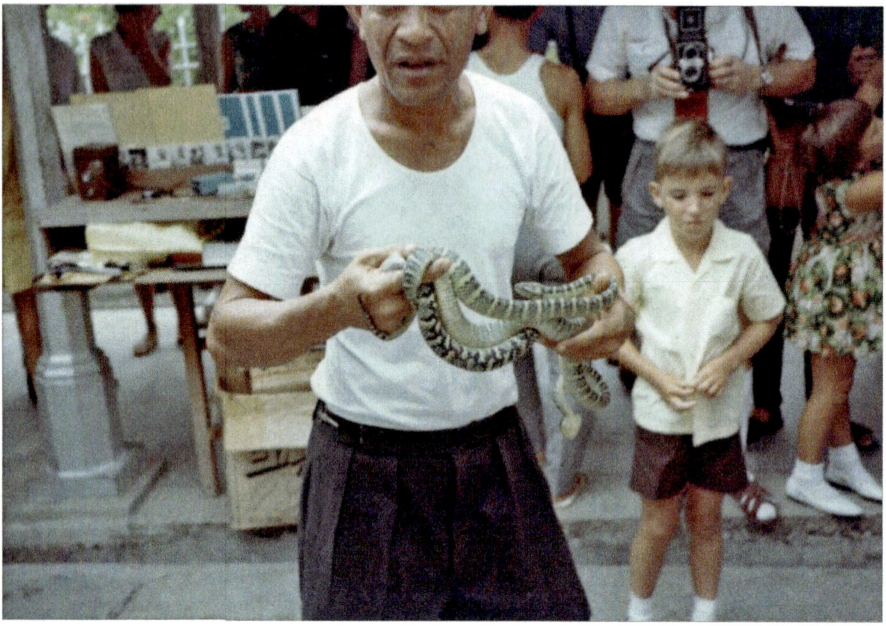

And, speaking of snakes, the next stop on the tour was a beach where a few snake charmers performed traditional snake charming routines, coaxing hooded cobras out of baskets by playing on bulbous flute-like instruments. Of course, it was something of a tourist trap, so, as expected, we dropped some cash into one of the baskets that didn't contain a cobra.

The Snake Temple wasn't the only "must-see" thing on Penang. There was, and probably still is, a funicular railway that took passengers to the top of Penang Hill, some 2,700 feet high. We took the trip up there and were rewarded by the pleasantly cool, non-humid air that was a welcome escape from the stifling heat that we had been subjected to for the past nearly two years. It was even a surprise to see a rose garden up there because rose bushes just don't tolerate the tropical heat they would experience at lower altitudes in that part of the world.

When we had travelled to Penang, it had been via Kuala Lumpur, the capital of Malaysia, and it was the same route on the way back, so we decided to stop over for a day and take a look around. We booked into the Railway Hotel because it was less expensive than some of the others we tried. It turned out to be a relic of the colonial era, and there was no doubt it had seen much better days during that period. The room we were given had a high ceiling with a lazily turning fan to keep the air circulating, but it smelled musty. The wallpaper was peeling, and the en suite bathroom fixtures would have seemed familiar to the likes of Somerset Maugham. We only stayed there one night – and that was far too long.

The next day we looked around for a while before going to the airport. The only thing that sticks in my mind was the minaret of a newly built mosque that was designed to resemble a space rocket. The airport was also remarkable. It had been recently built in a grand architectural style to lure international airlines away from Singapore, but alas it didn't work, so the Malaysians were left with a huge, beautiful airport that only catered for MSA, while Singapore's Paya Lebar airport still handled the bulk of flights to that part of the world.

Chapter 16: Repatriation

Back in our Rose Garden flat, it was time to think about getting our belongings packed up, mostly things we had acquired during our stay, ready for shipment back to Blighty. We hadn't overdone it, concentrating more on saving up to buy a house when we got home, but there were a few things we had definitely wanted to acquire. One prized possession was a Noritake dinner service, and then there was the Sony reel-to-reel tape recorder that we had used to record messages for home. But it was also great for playing the collection of music tapes we had built up. I haven't mentioned this before, but one of the things that certain merchants in Changi Village would do for a modest consideration was make recordings of popular LP records onto tape. That way, customers such as me and countless other servicemen, could have high-fidelity copies of the records for a lot less than the LP itself would have cost. I had made frequent use of this service and certainly wanted to take the tapes home with me. There was also a set of solid teak table lamps and a standard lamp. The standard lamp was designed to break down into three separate pieces for the sole purpose of being able to be packed for shipment. These had been made for us by a local entrepreneur who turned the wood on a lathe and then hand carved the intricate designs into the wood.

As with postings in the U.K. for married personnel, the Service footed the bill for a removal company to pack and move household belongings from the old location to the new one. All that a serviceman needed to do was submit three competing bids for the job to the Families Office and the least expensive bidder would be given the green light. The same was true for overseas postings and repatriations, except in those situations, a shipping company was involved. But, just as in the U.K., any shipping company that was approached obligingly offered to obtain the two other competing bids as a convenience. It was no big surprise that the two other bids were always higher. We selected a shipping company and received all three bids, which I dutifully submitted for approval. A few days later, two Chinese men knocked on our door and said they were here to pack our belongings and get them to the shipper. It was rare to see an overweight Chinese man or woman in Singapore, but one of these men had the body shape of a Buddha statue. In the meantime, we had moved everything that we wanted to take back with us into the living room and so they got to work. The two sat themselves on the living room floor, surrounded by the small items to be packed, and set about preparing them for the sea journey. Every small item was carefully wrapped and placed in a wooden crate. All the while, the two chatted and joked with each other in Chinese and completely ignored Pam and me. Sometimes they would burst out in peals of laughter, and I couldn't help wondering if maybe we, or some of our possessions, were the object of the joke. It's like that old joke saying, "It's not that I'm paranoid; it's just that I just know they're out to get me!"

After two days, everything was packed in two wooden shipping crates, which the men manoeuvred down the three flights of stairs and into their lorry. We wouldn't see the crates for several weeks after we arrived back home, but there was nothing in them that we desperately needed. We had already sold the TV set and any other items we didn't want to take with us or gave them to our amah. The next step now was to "march out" of the flat, which, if I can respectfully remind you, was a Hiring. We went around to make sure everything was clean and that nothing was broken. Then, on the appointed day, a civilian from the Families Office came to the door. He studiously inspected the entire house, but we were confident that everything was clean and in good order. But we were wrong! In the bathroom, he peered closely at the washbasin, and then got closer to it until his head was nearly in the bowl. After a few moments of this strange behaviour, he straightened up and announced that the basin was cracked.

"What?" I exclaimed.

He pointed to what looked like a fine hair on the porcelain surface. I saw it and tried to brush it away, but it wasn't a hair, it was a hairline crack. We had never dropped anything into the washbasin, so I could only assume that it was there when we took the flat over, and told him so, but he was deaf to our protests. The result was that we were charged an exorbitant price for a replacement washbasin. I would be willing to bet my life that that washbasin was never replaced and if any poor sod took on the Hiring after us, he would have been the victim of the same experience.

Prior to "marching out," we had checked into "Changi Creek" on the edge of Changi Village. This was the transit accommodation for families and a far cry from the transit billet where I had stayed on first arriving, when I was on my unaccompanied way to Labuan. No, it was nothing like that transit billet and the strangeness I had experienced there but was more like a small private hotel. The lodging, the food, the staff, and the amenities were excellent. We would spend two or three days there until it was time to board our repatriation flight. We had nothing to do but relax and wander around the village. The only duty I needed to perform was to clear from RAF Changi. This took me to my old section where the lads presented me with a pewter mug inscribed with my name and the station badge. Of course, I would expect you to believe that this was in acknowledgement of my incredible popularity by a group of hero-worshipping underlings, but I hate to disillusion you. In fact, it was no surprise to be presented with the mug because all my previous colleagues had also received one on the occasion of their repatriation. Those us who wanted to receive this beautiful souvenir at the end of our tour, and most did, had contributed a small sum to the kitty each payday that paid for the mug and its inscription. It was a welcome keepsake that I still cherish and use for the occasional adult beverage.

On August 16th, 1968, we boarded an MT bus for transportation to the Station Flight departure lounge. It was nostalgic in many ways. I gazed out of the bus window at the familiar sights that I had become used to over the nearly two years I had spent there. There was the Electronics Squadron on the left, the post office a little further along on the right, the main gate where the local SP stamped around on his wooden box, directing the traffic, last on the route was The Chartered Bank, which had taken good care of our savings during my tour. The bus then turned off the Changi Road and arrived at the departure lounge. Our aircraft was already there. No British Eagle Britannia going back – this was an Air Support Command Super VC10. We boarded when the call came and took our backwards-facing seats. There were no delays, unlike the time when I was on Station Flight duty and when we had been bollocked for coming on board to fix a snag before the passengers had disembarked. That time, it was dark when their VC10 took off, but we were on time and took off during daylight. I was impressed at how little noise there was from the engines as we lifted off and the flight was so smooth. This was certainly the way to travel!

The first stop was Gan, that lonely island in the middle of the Indian Ocean where those unluckier than me had to spend a one-year unaccompanied tour. We had passed into darkness by that time, so there was nothing to see of the island except the pan into which we taxied which was paved with crushed coral, giving it a white appearance. A quick turnaround and then we were off again, next stop Cyprus.

Naturally, at certain times during the flight, I had reason to visit the toilet at the rear of the passenger cabin. While in there taking care of business, I eyed the fake "NO SMOKING" sign up on the bulkhead. The little boy in me was sorely tempted to press it to unlatch the folding wall, but my adult self's good sense and maturity prevailed, so I was able to resist.

By the time we reached the general area of Cyprus, we were back to daylight. As we cruised high above what appeared to be desert country below, the overhead speakers crackled as one of the flight deck members made an announcement over the public address system. The nearest speaker to our seats was some distance away with the result that the announcement was almost unintelligible. I could only make out a few words – "descent" and "very noisy." The announcement clicked off with a 'pop' and almost immediately the VC10 went into what felt like a forty-five-degree steep descent, although it probably wasn't quite that steep. This was accompanied by a lot of noise and vibration which I took to be the engine reverse thrust being engaged. However, since then, I have been assured by several people that reverse thrust was never used by RAF aircrews on the VC10 to reduce airspeed, and that the noise and vibration was due solely to the spoilers and flaps being deployed. I take that as gospel, but whatever method was employed, the white-knuckle ride lasted for what seemed an eternity. Eventually, we levelled out at a much lower altitude and landed at Nicosia airport in Cyprus a short time later. I can only surmise that the steep descent was employed to avoid flying through unfriendly airspace, possibly Egyptian, but that's just a guess.

We were in a military aircraft, after all, so probably someone down below had an objection to the RAF transiting their airspace.

It was a surprise to land at a civilian airport. I had thought that RAF Akrotiri would have been our refuelling stop, but there may have been some reason for the diversion to Nicosia. It was quite early in the Cyprus morning when we landed and, stepping out of the aircraft, the air felt cool, clear and a very welcome breath of fresh air. A small fleet of buses ferried us and our fellow passengers to a transit lounge from where we had a grandstand view of the airport operations. Olympic Airways jets taxied back and forth, some going out to the runway for take-off, while others were coming in from the airfield, having just landed, at the same time, airport buses disgorged other travellers at the steps to the aircraft on which they would be flying. Time passed quickly and it was soon time to reboard for the final leg of the journey. This time the destination was RAF Lyneham.

* * *

The VC10 started to gently lose altitude over the English Channel so that when we made landfall we were, I would guess, at about 10,000 feet. The view below was a welcome sight – a beautiful patchwork of green and golden fields separated by darker hedgerows, all bathing in the bright mid-August sunshine. There were a few puffy, white clouds floating below us, like cottonwool balls, that cast their shadows on the otherwise sunlit ground. It was a sight for sore eyes!

The descent continued until we gently touched down at Lyneham. As the aircraft taxied to the terminal, we could see friends and family gathered in an area near where we would deplane. Many were waving, but we couldn't make out Pam's parents, who were supposed to be there to meet us and take us to their home. First, we needed to collect our luggage and duty-free stuff before passing through Customs, but with that done, we emerged from the terminal building to be greeted by Pam's parents, Ken and Doris. Hugs, kisses, and handshakes ensued before they ushered us to their car. They had thoughtfully brought coats for both of us, which were welcome, because even though it was a beautiful summer day, it felt chilly to Pam and me.

I had requested the Lincoln area for my final posting, but instead of returning to Waddington, as I would have wished, the posting was back to Scampton and the Gin Palace. We stayed with Ken and Doris for a few days, but when we had recovered sufficiently from our jet lag, we set about finding and renting a furnished flat in the city.

Eventually, we used the money we had saved up during our tour to put a deposit on a newly built bungalow in the village of Cherry Willingham, where we had lived prior to me being posted to Labuan. We had saved enough to completely furnish it with a fair amount still left in the bank. Surprisingly, the bargaining skills we had acquired in Singapore turned out to be very useful when buying expensive items like furniture and carpeting. When quoted a price, I always asked if that was the "best price" if we paid cash instead of buying with hire-purchase. The various merchants were always willing to negotiate with the result that we saved a fair amount just by using this tactic. I didn't need to use it just yet to buy a car because we hadn't wanted to give up our Austin Farina while we were overseas, so when Pam got the notification to come out to join me, she rented a vacant garage from one of the other bungalow dwellers where we had previously lived in Cherry Willingham. Pam's dad put the car up on blocks in the rented garage, removed the battery, drained the petrol tank, and then covered it with dust sheet. Periodically, he visited the garage to check on it, but otherwise, it remained safe in that locked garage until we got it out and brought it back to life.

Although we had been repatriated early because my 10-year engagement was nearing its completion, I signed on for another two years shortly after returning to Scampton. Basically, converting my two years of "reserve" service into actual service. This was so that I could attend the local Lincoln College of Technology to acquire an Ordinary National Certificate, or ONC as it was more commonly known, which I had soon discovered was absolutely necessary if I wanted to get a halfway decent job in Civvy Street. Then, four years later, as a civilian, I was finally able to cross that "bridge too far" when I gained an HNC, which I had started studying for as soon as I had achieved the ONC. It had seemed such an impossible goal back in the not-so-distant past, when I had asked that engineering officer in the Changi Education Centre how to become an engineer, but it turned out to be a case of just putting one foot in front of the other to get there.

Well, that ends my story of an overseas tour that began as an unaccompanied, one-year posting to Labuan, but ended up as an accompanied tour at Changi in Singapore. I hope you found it interesting, or perhaps even nostalgically memory-evoking if you too spent any time in the Far East.

Epilogue

Twenty years later, in June 1988, I returned to Singapore for the first time since leaving it all those years ago on that VC10. This time it was as a civilian to participate in an engineering meeting with a client company. What a different place I found it to be! Yet, it was still Singapore.

I landed at the same airfield from which I had departed in '68, but what had been RAF Changi then was now Singapore Changi Airport, and it was an airport to put most others in the world to shame.

Prior to my arrival, I had done a little research, hoping to visit some of our old haunts. I discovered that there was a Le Meridien Hotel outside what had been the back gate to the station – the one that led to the RAF Hospital on the station grounds. It had also been a secure area because there had been three or four "safe houses" inside the gate to which important Singapore government officials could be hustled in the event of civil strife that threatened their wellbeing, although that never happened during my time there.

Anyway, I took a taxi to Le Meridien, having made a prior reservation, and checked in. Having just flown in from Tokyo, where I had been attending a meeting with a different client, I wasn't feeling jet lagged and it still being early in the day, I decided to take a look around. The first port of call was nearby Changi village, and what a disappointment. The entire village had been rebuilt in uniform red brick, with two or three floors of flats above the ground floor shops. The individuality expressed by the uneven, rickety architecture of the shops and buildings that had characterized the old village had been completely lost in its now blanket uniformity.

Next, I set off walking along the old Changi Road that led away from the village when Changi was a RAF station. In those days it was heavily travelled by all manner of traffic, but now it was eerily quiet. I passed my old workplace, the Electronics Squadron. The building was still there, but access was denied by a sturdy metal grilled gate topped with a reel of barbed wire. Continuing on along the road, I passed what remained of the post office, but it had been repurposed for something else. Further on, I passed the T-junction that led to the main camp entrance, where the local SP used to stamp his feet on the wooden box as he performed parade square turns to direct the traffic. The box was gone, as was the SP, but so was the traffic.

By this time, I was getting an eerie feeling of being some kind of departed spirit that had returned to haunt the location of his former life. Probably not far from the truth, except that I was still a flesh and bone human being. Further on, I wanted to see the pan and the barrier that used to close Changi Road off to traffic when aircraft needed to taxi across to and from the runway, but as I approached it was apparent that this was the end of the line because a chain-link fence that stretched all the way across the road barred my way.

As I turned around to walk back to the hotel, a military Land Rover came belting around the curve from the direction of the village and pulled up alongside me. Without getting out of the vehicle, one of the two men in military uniform asked me in a reasonably polite, but no-nonsense manner, what I was doing in that area which, he said was restricted. I explained that I had been stationed there while in the RAF back in the 1960s and wanted to see how it all looked now. On telling him this, I expected that the nostalgia obviously inherent in my explanation would be met with a little understanding, but there was none. He just said that I needed to turn around and go back the way I had come. So, I started walking, thinking that maybe they would give me a lift, but no, the Land Rover just crept along a few feet behind me until I was halfway back to the village, when they apparently decided I was no longer a security risk.

The next day, I took a taxi into the city to attend the engineering meeting, which is why I was there in the first place. Instead of taking me along Changi Road, as would have been the route in the old days, and which was now impassable, as I had discovered the previous day, the cab headed towards the airport complex to join up with a wide motorway that was equal to any motorway or freeway in the western world. It was neat and clean with colourful bougainvillea and other attractive vegetation growing along its sides and hanging from the overpasses. This left me with the impression that Singapore had turned itself into a garden city.

That evening, after taking my customers to dinner at a posh restaurant on Orchard Road, (well, somebody had to do it), I noticed the sophisticated appearance of an affluent group of young Singaporeans. They were dressed in fashionable western clothing, the young women elegantly made up and sporting fashionable hair styles. I noticed they were coming out of an underground railway station, which was something that hadn't been there during the British presence. Lee Kwan Yoo's fears for the City State, when the British pulled out, turned out to be unfounded. He had obviously found a way for Singapore to flourish and prosper.

I was travelling alone, which was unusual. Another of my company's engineers had been supposed to join me in Singapore to participate in the meeting but had been diverted elsewhere. This gave me a free hand to fudge on when to return to the home office, so I decided to stay another day and do some more exploration of the places that had been familiar to Pam and me when we had lived there. The best way to do that, I thought, was to hire a taxi and explain to the driver what I wanted to do. Luckily, the driver of the taxi I picked was intelligent, and chatty in an informational way. I explained about my service in Singapore and that I wanted to visit Katong because of having lived there. He surprised me by saying that he had been a police officer at a sub-station in Katong around the time Pam and I had lived there and knew it well.

On arriving in the Katong area, the first thing I noticed was that the Rose Garden complex was still there, although it appeared to be a little shabbier than when we lived there. The other surprising thing was that the neighbouring kampong was no more, and in its place were a number of large, expensive-looking houses. I remarked on this to the driver, who replied that the kampong inhabitants had been rooted out of their homes and forced to move into flats in the multi-storey, high rise buildings that dotted the area. The land had then been used for these exclusive houses to be built for the very rich and influential Singaporeans. He went on to say that there were no kampongs on Singapore island anymore and that the former kampong people hated the high-rise towers in which they had been relocated, because it was the death knell for the community relationships they had grown up enjoying.

This prompted a discussion of how the ordinary Singaporeans liked their modern government. He remarked that working class people were generally unhappy, mainly because they were forced to live like battery hens. Having heard that Singapore had an exceptionally low crime rate compared to that of the western world, I offered that as a plus, but he blew that off by saying that the government monitored every aspect of the citizens' lives and that they did not enjoy the freedom that we in the west take for granted. That was a surprise!

Driving further into Katong, it was noticeable that the big, ugly, rat and cockroach infested monsoon drains had been paved over and most of the open-fronted shops and cooking establishments had been replaced by shops that wouldn't have looked too out of place on a British street. It was all remarkably cleaner as well. We continued along the East Coast Road up to Bedok Junction. The little beach where Pam and I had often sunbathed and swam was no more. Land reclamation had already taken it shortly before we had been repatriated. Now, there was a golf course there and the whole area had been built up with affluent shopping arcades and expensive flats. Eventually, the driver dropped me off at my hotel where I thanked him, gave him a good tip, and we said goodbye.

The next day, I went to the airport for my flight home. The departure lounge, which I hadn't seen when I arrived, was impressive. I found it to be a long concourse, spotlessly clean and paved with gleaming ceramic tiles. Along the way, the kind of shops that can be found in most western duty-free areas lined the concourse, selling all kinds of expensive consumer goods – cameras, watches, jewellery, perfumes, clothing and so on. I tried to work out which area of the old airfield it occupied and came to the conclusion, rightly or wrongly, that the footprint it occupied had been the approximate location of the RAF Jungle Survival Training School on the far side of the RAF era airfield. At least, that's how it appeared. Also, the runway had been lengthened to accommodate the larger, wide-body aircraft that were now the airport's main clientele.

Soon, my boarding call came, and I was on my way back to San Diego. That had been the first time I had returned, but there were two other business trips back there before I retired. Each of the subsequent times, I came with a few others, all of us members of a project team, so I never had the opportunity to do any more exploring by myself. But on this first occasion, I think I had seen enough and left with mixed feelings – glad that Singapore had successfully made its way in the world, but a little sad that the people were not so happy with the status quo. But then again, isn't that human nature?

Photo Credits

British Eagle Britannia – *Provided by Air Team Images*

Basha huts – *Courtesy of Boy Entrant 40th Entry website*

Twin Pioneer – *Provided by Radfanhunters.co.uk*

Single Pioneer – *Air Team Images*

HP Hastings - *Wikipedia.org/wiki/No._48_Squadron_RAF*

Argosy – *Original version provided by John Phillips.*

Asian Toilet – *Courtesy www.travel.stackexchange.com*

Airport terminal, Labuan – *Courtesy of North Borneo Historical Scty.*

Cambodian Air Force DC3 - *Courtesy of Boy Entrant 40th Entry website https://www.40thcosford.org.uk/Labuan_page1.htm*

Trumpetfish – *Brittanica.com/Animal/Trumpetfish, Image: Jan Derk*

Changi barrack block – *Rememberingsingapore.wordpress.com*

Yellowtop (Pick-up) taxis – *Facebook Group "Nostalgic Singapore."*

Chinese weight scale – *AliExpress.com*

Katong (today) – *Google Earth screen capture*

Malay wedding couple – *Pinterest.co.uk*

BOAC VC 10 (The Moonlighter) – *Provided by AirTeamImages*

Wayang performers – *Wikipedia*

Thaipusam – *Wikipedia*

Acknowledgements

The content in this book has mostly been drawn from my personal memories reinforced by a fair amount of research, however, I did receive help in a few different ways from others.

Ian Duckham, Steve Lister and Brian Peacock for providing photos by way of the *Boy Entrant 40th Entry website, (https://www.40thcosford.org.uk/Labuan_page1.htm)*. And to Ian Duckham for his recollection of moving into the Sergeants Mess at Labuan when he and a few others remained at the end.

Hally Hardie, former 81 Squadron navigator, for his help and support in attempting to get to the bottom of the visiting Canberra P7.

David Marinholz for reminding me that I met Barry Goodall in Changi Village and not in Malta.

Ken Brererton for his humorous observation on the class of service provided on flights to and from Labuan.

David Holgate for his description of the Long Bar in Raffles.

Chris Webb for providing some insights into the SIB's activities in Singapore.

John Phillips for kindly permitting me to make changes to his Argosy photograph to fit it in with my narrative.

My daughter, Michelle for proof-reading the final manuscript, and her help in designing the cover layout.

And last, but not least, Paul Seymour for the excellent cover art, specially commissioned for this book.

About The Author

A native of Coleraine, Northern Ireland in February 1941, I joined the Royal Air Force as a boy entrant in October 1956, four months prior to my sixteenth birthday, to train as an Electrical Mechanic (Air). For the next 18 months, I underwent the rigours of military and technical training, graduating in the closing days of March 1958. I was then posted to the Royal Air Force College Cranwell (Flying Training Command, and for the next four years was engaged in servicing Vampires, Meteors, Jet Provosts and Chipmunks.

In April 1962, with the rank of Junior Technician, I was selected to participate in RAF's trials of the American made Skybolt air-launched ballistic missile with which the Vulcan V-bomber was to be armed. The trials were to be held at the USAF Eglin Air Force Base in Florida. In order to gain familiarization with the Vulcan, I was attached to Bomber Command's 230 Operational Conversion Unit at RAF Finningley, Yorkshire.

Unfortunately for me, Skybolt programme and associated trials was cancelled in December 1962. Therefore, instead of going to sunny Florida, I was posted to RAF Waddington in March 1963 to serve on 50 Squadron, which was equipped with Vulcans. In June 1964, while still at Waddington, my fiancée Pam and I were married. A short time later, in October, I was selected to participate in the Kestrel Tripartite Evaluation Squadron.

At the conclusion of the Kestrel Evaluation Trials, I returned to Bomber Command and the Vulcans, but this time it was to RAF Scampton in February 1966. However, in October of the same year, I was then posted overseas to RAF Labuan, Borneo. But just two months later the "unaccompanied" posting was changed to an "accompanied" tour at Changi in Singapore and I was then able to bring Pam out to join me.

On repatriation, it was back to RAF Scampton, where I served out the remainder of my time in the RAF, attaining the rank of Sergeant several months before becoming a civilian "Mr." on 16th of February 1971. While working as an Electrical Draughtsman for the Ruston Gas Turbines Ltd company, based in the City of Lincoln, I continued with the four-year course of study at Lincoln College of Technology that I had started two years prior to leaving the RAF, finally graduating in 1972 with a Higher National Certificate in Electrical & Electronic Engineering. Meanwhile, our two daughters Michelle and Sarah were born, arriving in 1971 and 1973 respectively.

The prospect of higher financial reward lured me into signing up for a one-year contract as a Project Engineer with the Arabian American Oil Company (ARAMCO) in Saudi Arabia. Just like my RAF "unaccompanied" overseas posting to Labuan, the contract was "bachelor status," but I was able get to come home on leave every three months.

On returning to Lincoln and the family, my old firm, Ruston, offered me a position at their Houston, Texas, branch, Ruston Gas Turbines Inc., which I gratefully accepted. Eventually, I accepted a position with Solar Turbines Incorporated another industrial gas turbine company, initially as a Project Engineer in Houston. In 1985, the company transferred me to its home base in San Diego, California, with promotion to Project Manager.

In May 1992, as a family, we became American citizens and I remained with Solar Turbines for a total of 19 years before retiring in the year 2000, having achieved the position of Principal Project Manager. I am content to live out my days in San Diego where our two daughters and five grandchildren also reside.

Printed in Great Britain
by Amazon